D0119872

A Garden of Herbs

A Garden
of Herbs

TRADITIONAL USES OF HERBS
IN SCOTLAND

Dr Agnes Walker

Argyll
publishing

First published in 2003 by
Argyll Publishing
Glendaruel
Argyll PA22 3AE
Scotland
www.skoobe.biz

Acknowledgement is made to the Professor
Lloyd Binns Bequest Fund, administered by
the Glasgow Natural History Society for
financial support in producing this book.

**British Library Cataloguing-in-Publication
Data.**
**A catalogue record for this book is
available from the British Library.**

ISBN 1 902831 55 1

Origination: Cordfall Ltd, Glasgow

Printing: Cromwell Press Ltd, Wiltshire

To family and friends
who have helped
make this book possible

Contents

Echinacea
This plant is considered
by many herbalists to be
one of the most
important immune
stimulants in Western
herbal medicine. It
should not, however, be
taken if on other
medication

Helen Abdy

Preface

There seems to be a never-ending demand for books on cooking, on maintaining good health and on gardening. We are all interested in good, nutritious food, staying healthy for as long as possible and many of us love gardening. Here is a book which tells us about culinary plants, about the beneficial properties of herbs and about herb gardens.

Why is this book different from the many others which deal with these matters? Firstly, it has a strong Scottish flavour and the section on the ancient Highland medical tradition reveals the advanced state of medical knowledge, derived from far afield as well as from the local plant lore; this knowledge had existed for a long time before the dissolution of the clan system after the mid eighteenth century. Secondly, Agnes Walker is very careful to point out the potential dangers of using herbs unwisely. Thirdly, there is reference to the archaeological records of culinary or medicinal plants from Scottish and foreign sites and this shows just how long-standing such uses are.

Few Scots will have heard of the Highland dynasties of physicians such as the Beatons, who for hundreds of years were doctors to the Scottish Kings and the Lords of the Isles. Few Scots or visitors will know of the use of coriander, as a spice or a medicine, by the Roman troops when they occupied the fort at Bearsden, northwest of Glasgow, nearly two thousand years ago. In this engaging little book you can read about these and other matters as well about dye plants and aromatic and cosmetic herbs.

James H. Dickson
Professor of Archaeobotany and Plant Systematics
University of Glasgow

Acknowledgements

The late Professor John Lenihan gave me encouragement to write this book, but the real incentive came from a visit to Timespan Heritage Museum herb garden at Helmsdale in Sutherland, where Mrs Mary Dudgeon and some of her friends have created a delightful small herb garden.

I have had practical help from the staff of the Glasgow Botanic Gardens, and many of the plants I have written of are in their new herb garden. Two paintings are by Helen Abdy, one of a group of artists who take inspiration from the gardens, and have regular exhibitions in the Visitors Centre.

I have had generous help in botanical and pharmaceutical matters from JH Dickson, Professor of Archeobotany and Plant Systematics, University of Glasgow and JD Phillipson, Emeritus Professor, The School of Pharmacy, University of London. I have consulted Dr Margaret Mackay of the School of Scottish Studies, Edinburgh University, where there is a fascinating record of the traditional uses of many of the herbs of which I have written.

I cannot speak highly enough of my friends, Maggie Anderson, Sheila Jennett, Janet Jones, Irene Nove, Jean Reid, Edna Robertson, Ursula Cairns-Smith, Barbara Sumner and Suzanne Ullmann, who read my later drafts and Betty Knott-Sharp, who advised on classical history and its writers; also Dee Atkinson of Napier's, Herbalists, who gave useful advice and Anita Pearman who painted some herbs not in *British Wild Flowers* by Sowerby & Johnson where most illustrations are from.

To members of the Glasgow Natural History Society, who commented on my early drafts, especially Professor Norman Grist, who gave me encouragement and advice on medical aspects of the work, Morag Mackinnon and Pearl Tait for advice on the process of dyeing, I am most grateful. Also to the Professor Blodwen Lloyd Binns Bequest Fund, administered by the Glasgow Natural History Society, which has made money available towards the printing of the book to help keep the price at what I hope will make it accessible to visitors to herb gardens.

Agnes Walker BSc, MSc, PhD, MIBiol

April 2003

Introduction

What are herbs? By a strict botanical definition they are non-woody plants that grow from seeds, flower, and produce seeds that ripen and then grow into next year's plants. But a broader definition, as used in most books about herbs, includes certain woody shrubs and trees and even non-flowering plants such as lichens and fungi. I have used this broader definition.

On a visit to the delightful herb garden at Timespan Heritage Centre in Helmsdale, Sutherland, I was so amazed by the range of herbs being grown so far north that I was inspired to write a book about them. This accorded well with an earlier suggestion by the late Professor John Lenihan, that, with my medical and botanical background, I should write about how traditional usage of herbs could be integrated with modern research. People now are very much aware of how herbs are used to improve the flavour and digestibility of food and television has shown us how to achieve beautiful gardens in which plants look and smell good. With more leisure time an interest in hand-dyeing of wool using plants has increased.

Herbs have suddenly become big business and a myth has been promulgated that all 'natural' herbs are safe. This is not always true. The fact that more and more people have become interested in self-treatment with herbs made me feel that there exists a need to be informed about what it is they are using. There is evidence expressed by some respected scientists that some herbal remedies are safer than conventional drugs but people should always consult a health-care professional, either their doctor or a medical herbalist, before using complementary medicines, especially if they are pregnant or on prescribed drugs.

Everyone knows what kind of expertise to expect from their doctor but it is not widely known that the professional medical herbalist is also trained in diagnostic skills, and aspires, in common with the best orthodox medical tradition, to a holistic approach to illness. According to a recent survey in Scotland most general practitioners believe this approach to be essential for good healthcare.* Although there have been no large clinical trials in herbal treatments, careful review of very long-established protocols and the collation of results obtained over many generations can be analysed by modern statistical methods. The results are often encouraging.

Another aim of this book is to make people aware of the range and depth of knowledge of the old Scottish physicians who studied the remedies and translated the manuscripts of renowned Arab and Greek physicians attached to the great medieval universities of Salerno and Montpellier. They added their own medical wisdom which was mainly herbal. Little is known, even in Scotland, of the legacy in the medieval medicinal Gaelic manuscripts held in the National Library of Scotland. Even the World Health Organisation, which collects traditional medicines from many countries, appears to have neglected our own valuable Scottish heritage.

The herbs selected here are those you would find growing in a typical Scottish herb garden together with herbs that are commonly for sale in herb shops, garden centres or supermarkets. A few more exotic herbs that are grown in some herb gardens, either in a glasshouse or a cold frame, because they have an important role in herbal medicine in our country have been added. I have traced the long history of these herbs and described their uses in the light of present-day knowledge.

I hope that this book will help you to learn more about the herbs our ancestors used in cooking, in other crafts and in medicine. I trust it will help bridge the gap between scientific pharmaceutical books and popular books on the uses of medicinal herbs and I hope you will enjoy reading it as much as I have enjoyed the research.

I have included numbered references to my sources in the text which refer to the bibliography on page 117. An asterisk in the text refers to notes at the end of each section.

Herbs are described under several headings, some of them appearing in more than one section.

In each section the herbs are listed alphabetically under their botanical, ie Latin names, which allows similar plants to be grouped together, however an English/Latin index is on page 109. There is a glossary of botanical and medical terms.

Where there is a specific Scottish use, this is mentioned in the text, since the intention was to use this book when visiting herb gardens in Scotland. A few non-flowering plants such as lichens have been included because of their interesting historical usage in Scotland.

The names of herbs are as in Bown[7] and Stace.[52] Some of the herbs described are hybrids and these are denoted by an 'x' in the botanical name. A 'v' in the botanical name denotes a particular variety of the species described.

British Medical Journal 2002 vol. 325

Calendula
Marigold is one of the
most useful herbs in
Western medicine.
Known in Scotland by
995AD and used
continuously since, it is
frequently used as a
remedy for most minor
skin problems.

14   *A Garden of Herbs*

1.
Herbs and Medicine

Henbane

At the dawn of medical knowledge is the important figure of the Egyptian, Imhotep who lived at the beginning of the third millenium BC.* He was considered the 'Father of Medicine' and was worshipped as a healer and a god for over 2000 years (from 2850 to 525BC) and as a full deity until 550AD. He was also known as an astrologer and magician, medicine and magic being linked together in belief and practice. He urged contentment, preached cheerfulness and coined the saying 'eat, drink and be merry for tomorrow we shall die'.

Imhotep extracted curative agents from plants including henbane and wormwood and he treated many diseases such as tuberculosis, appendicitis and arthritis with herbs. Physicians were very important people and the hieroglyph for a physician was a seated figure with an arrow and a cooking pot, and it is of interest to note that there was even a separate one for a woman doctor! By about 1,500BC the Egyptians had listed on a papyrus more than 850 plant medicines. Their pharmacopoeia included garlic, aloe, castor oil, opium and mandrake, which most Egyptologists believe to have been the magical substance called the elixir of life. The knowledge of Egyptian medicine is derived from various papyruses, *eg* the Ebers papyrus which tells us that opium and mandrake were manufactured into intoxicating and narcotic drinks. **

Some believe the fruits of mandrake to have been the Biblical love-apples eaten by Leah and Rachel (Genesis XXX, 14) as a pregnancy charm, and, although, this has been disputed, it has been asserted that in the early 1900s Jewish and Moslem women still purchased mandrakes in Palestine.*** In India the Vedas, epic poems written *c.*1500BC (although recent research suggests that these may be of much earlier origin) contain information on many herbs, and this forms the basis of the Ayurvedic system of medicine still practised throughout India today.

A Chinese Emperor is credited with writing the first real herbal dealing with the preparation and uses of medicinal plants. This fine illustrated herbal dates from about 1000BC. In it 365 plants are described, some well known to us, *eg* opium and ephedra and others less familiar like Kalaw seeds. Kalaw was re-discovered by western medicine in the nineteenth century to be the first successful treatment for leprosy and is still in use today. There is an extraordinary continuity over the centuries in the methodology of Chinese herbal medicine, many of the procedures, *eg* acupuncture, introduced by the early physicians are still used.

Egypt was absorbed into the Greek cultured world in the fourth century BC and the Greeks who lived there adopted the worship of Imhotep. They identified him with their own native healer, Asclepius, son of Apollo, the god of healing and destruction. Asclepius was already well-known as a physician in the Homeric poems. He came to be considered semi-divine, and acquired several shrines and healing centres in the Greek world, the most important being at Epidauros. An important part of the healing was 'incubation', *ie* sleeping in a special part of the precinct. This was preceded by sacrifice and purification and accompanied by symbolic rituals. It was expected that the god would meet with the patient and reveal the appropriate treatment in a dream. One cannot help but wonder what drugs and herbs were used in inducing the dreams and in the healing processes.

Hippocrates, known today as the 'Father of Medicine' and originator of the Hippocratic Oath, lived in the fifth century BC. The considerable body of medical works attributed to him includes a scientific system of medicine and rejects magic. The Hippocratic Oath was until recently sworn to by new medical graduands.

In the first century AD a Greek physician, Dioscorides, wrote his large *De Materia Medica*, an authoritative study of herbal medicines and a standard reference work throughout the Middle Ages. He described some six hundred plants with their uses including some used today like chamomile, marjoram, thyme and rhubarb. He also advised on the use of plants for abortion and contraception; the plant he used is found today to be effective in preventing pregnancy.

About the same time the Roman polymath and encyclop-
aedist Pliny, the Elder (23-79AD) wrote his vast *Naturalis Historia*,
and these included medicinal uses of plants. He reported that
the treatments he mentioned often cured illness, but did not
claim to know how they worked. He mentioned some Gallic
names of herbs,* for example *vela*, which probably means hedge
mustard (he says this is good, taken with honey, for coughs) and
vettonica which is betony, *Stachys officinalis*, one of the herbs included in this book. Ulcers were apparently treated successfully as
was scurvy by herbs such as scurvy grass, that contain vitamin C.

The earliest known herbal of British origin, the Saxon *Leech
Book of Bald*, written *c*.900AD, makes reference to remedies of
Scottish origin. By the twelfth century there were at least 150
hospitals attached to religious houses in Scotland. Herb gardens
were commonly associated with monastic orders as names like
bishop's-weed might suggest. (It is also called goutweed: one
wonders if this name tells us about some of the monk's foibles!)
Remains of medicinal plants have been found at the Scottish
religious houses at Whithorn (founded 5-600AD) and Paisley
Abbey (founded *c*.1165AD), including the powerful drug plant
hemlock.[14]

There have long been monastic herb gardens in Britain and
Europe, but later herb gardens were associated with universities,
the herbs being used, until very recently, for teaching medical
students. The one in Glasgow, founded in 1555, was a small
garden, near the old university, growing parsley, celery, pot
marigold, asparagus, fennel, valerian and other herbs.[6] The
garden in Edinburgh was established in 1670, by Dr (later Sir)
Robert Sibbald, founder (in 1681) of the Royal College of
Physicians. Now herb gardens are mainly preserved for popular
interest.

By the Middle Ages (*c*.1000-1400AD) many scholars, including women, had studied medicinal herbs. The German Abbess
Hildegard of Bingen is known to have used herbs. She believed
God had told her they were provided to heal and to protect
against illness. Today there is a fresh interest in some of her
remedies. In the late Middle Ages, it seems that the practice of
medicine abandoned rational science and people began to rely
on the Doctrine of Signatures. This 'Doctrine' stated that God
had ordained that if a herb looked like part of the body (ie its
'signature') it told the physician what the herb could be used to
treat. For example lungwort was considered to look like lobes

of the lung and so was used to treat lung disease.[38] This led to many strange remedies and for some time the earlier traditional herbs may have been neglected.

As this book is dealing with the Scottish medical tradition, a more extensive treatment of that tradition in the later Middle Ages and early modern times will be found in a later chapter.

About twenty-five per cent of all dispensed prescriptions currently contain an active ingredient of natural origin. Some prescription medicines contain substances isolated directly from plants, *eg digoxin* from foxgloves used to treat heart disease; the pain killer morphine, quinine from Peruvian bark; and codeine from the opium poppy. Knowledge of what plants contain has led to synthetic analogues. Many painkillers for example are based on the structure of morphine; some muscle relaxants are based on the active principal in *curare* (the South American arrow poison); yams, long used by African women to prevent pregnancy, are now used for the semi-synthesis of oral contraceptives.

Today there has been a resurgence of interest in traditional, long-respected herbs, and scientists are very involved with the collection of evidence for their usefulness. Some herbs, however, which are today sold over the counter have been shown to have potentially serious interactions with prescribed drugs, for example HIV treatments, and oral contraceptives. Among such are St John's wort, ginseng, garlic and valerian which interfere with a number of prescribed drugs.

People should always consult their doctors before using complementary medicines, if they are on other drugs. Conventional medicine is careful in prescribing any drug during pregnancy. Similar care must be taken when using herbal remedies. Even some herbal tea can be harmful if taken excessively during pregnancy, or when feeding a baby.

Most conventional drugs contain a pure chemical, not the complex group of chemicals as found in plants, although many modern drugs are purified substances that have been recognised as the active principle in herbal remedies and are extracted from the plants or copied by chemical synthesis. Herbalists believe that synergism occurs between the naturally-occurring chemicals. For example the ascorbic acid in citrus fruits is more available than in the 'manufactured' vitamin C. In herbal medicine controlled clinical trials to test the efficacy of drugs,

A Garden of Herbs

as in conventional medicine, does not take place, but analysis of exhaustive case histories over many years gives much confidence. Many established remedies have been used by millions of people since pre-history. It must be borne in mind that when any treatment is followed by a positive outcome (which might be due to natural recovery), this is always more likely to be remembered than a negative outcome. Only controlled trials, when one treatment is compared with another or with none, in large groups of patients, can logically establish a positive effect. Cures following uses of many different herbs over centuries has, however, often been vindicated by modern research. The medical herbalist uses a holistic approach where the patient's general state of health is dealt with as well as the symptoms being treated. The herbalist, like all medical doctors, uses all normal medical equipment and tests that may be necessary. [43]

Some herbalists even believe that there is a movement within drug companies to discredit alternative medicine. This may be because of the problems involved in the manufacture of pills or preparation of tinctures from plants. These procedures must always be carried out with scrupulous attention to methodology in order to obtain consistency and no loss in ingredients. There has been justified criticism in this area, but research into standardising procedures, eg period in the plant's growth cycle, time of day of collection (to take into account the plant's natural daily rhythm), storage, extraction procedures, etc are all essential in the preparation of standard doses and these variables are being addressed to rectify this.

extracts have been used to treat hypertension, and coronary thrombosis, but this use is not confirmed clinically, so care must be taken till these are known to be safe. A volatile oil, containing *azulines*, has been isolated from yarrow. *Azulines* are anti-inflammatory.[3] There is a suspicion yarrow can produce a light sensitive reaction, so extracts should be avoided if you intend to sunbathe.[3]

ACHILLEA MILLEFOLIUM
YARROW

Also known as *herba militaris*, yarrow has a long record as a healer of wounds. Achilles treated his warrior's wounds with it, hence its botanical name; and 'yarrow' comes from the Anglo-Saxon for 'healer'. In Scotland an ointment was made to heal and dry wounds and to treat piles. Fresh leaves were traditionally used to alleviate toothache.[5] Yarrow's bitter properties are said to help improve digestion by stimulating the secretion of gastric juices, as well as, supposedly, boosting liver, gall-bladder and kidney function. As with some members of the daisy family, yarrow may provoke an allergic reaction, *eg* dermatitis, in some people, so anyone with an existing sensitivity to members of this family should not even drink the herb tea. Yarrow was used to treat excessive menstruation,[12] but it must be avoided in pregnancy because of its reputed effect on the menstrual cycle and because of a reputation that it might cause abortion. Plant

ACONITUM NAPELLUS
MONK'S-HOOD WOLF'S-BANE

The whole plant is very poisonous; even skin contact can be dangerous.[39] It was a Chinese arrow poison, the toxin being the alkaloid *aconitine*.[53] In the late Middle Ages the Beatons* made use of it, but warned that great care was needed to find the correct dose.[2] It is still commonly grown as a decorative plant in the Highlands especially in Sutherland.[5] It is a potent painkiller, but is dangerous so must not be grown in a garden where children may play alone.

A Garden of Herbs

ACORUS CALAMUS
SWEET-FLAG

This ancient Eastern herb was mentioned in the Book of Exodus. Its dried roots were found among precious objects in the tomb of Tutankhamun (dating from c.1350BC). It was known in Britain from 1600AD, possibly earlier.[24] Traditionally it was regarded as an aphrodisiac, but the powdered dried rhizome (really an underground stem) was used as a mild sedative, as a stimulant for the salivary and gastric glands, and to treat colic and other minor stomach aches, as well as worms. The oil was used in the Highlands to reduce blood pressure.[5] The candied rhizome was popular in eighteenth century England as a medicinal lozenge to treat coughs and indigestion.[54] It is one of the most common herbs in Indian bazaars where it is sold to treat bruises and rheumatism.[24] Recent studies indicate that an oil from the rhizome in some members of this plant family is carcinogenic and may cause liver damage and possible convulsions,[44] but the American variety is said not to contain this oil, so this variety should be safe.[12]

ACTAEA SPICATA
BANEBERRY

It is very poisonous, as the 'bane' part of the name suggests. The powdered root is mildly sedative and is said to be a remedy for catarrh but should be used only under medical supervision.

AEGOPODIUM PODAGRARIA
GROUND-ELDER
BISHOP'S-WEED; GOUTWEED

Monks are said to have introduced ground-elder to Britain in the Middle Ages.[24] Its popular names invite the suspicion that it was used to treat bishops suffering from gout – it was certainly found near monasteries. In 1597, the herbalist Gerard also spoke of its diuretic and sedative effects and its virtues in curing gout; the cooked fresh root and leaf being eaten for gout and for aches in the joints. When leaves were applied directly, in cases of inflammation from sciatica and gout, the pain appeared to have been eased.[24]

Agrimony

AGRIMONIA EUPATORIA
AGRIMONY

The specific name(the second Latin name) refers to King Eupator, ancient King of Persia, who was renowned as a herbalist. The name 'agrimony' is a corruption of the Greek *argemon*, a white speck on the cornea of the eye. Eye problems were very

common in the East in biblical times; so this herb may have had an important role. It was also an ingredient of *eau de arquebusade*, an ointment used for healing battle wounds, from a fifteenth-century word for musket or *arquebus*. It had an early reputation for curing jaundice and other liver complaints and for treating blood diseases and ulcers.[24] It was used to treat liver problems by medical practioners in the Highlands.[5] Agrimony was collected and stored for winter use in the Highlands to make into tea for headaches.[48] Because of its potential as a healing herb a limited re-evaluation of it has been carried out and has indicated its healing properties in certain skin diseases and gastrointestinal disorders. Excessive use should be avoided, especially if you are using other drugs.[44]

AJUGA REPTANS
BUGLE

Extracts of the dried herb were once used to treat coughs and to stop haemorrhages. It was also said to combat the effects of over-drinking. In the European tradition bugle was long valued as a wound-healing herb and is still used occasionally for this purpose and as a mild analgesic.[12]

ALCHEMILLA VULGARIS
LADY'S-MANTLE

The 'Lady' is 'Our Lady', whose name is often associated with plants that were used to treat women's disorders; the leaves were said to look like her mantle. The root, powdered and mixed with red wine, was used as a skin lotion for cuts and abrasions; its infused green parts were used as a mouth rinse after tooth extraction and as a douche for vaginal infections. The plant's astringent effect is sufficiently marked that an infusion was used to contract the female genitals – very popular at one time with those wishing to appear to be virgins! It has been recommended that this should be avoided during pregnancy.[12]

ALGAE
SEAWEEDS

Various seaweeds have been important in Scotland – both for their mucilage, with its soothing effect on the stomach, and for their iodine content. The mucilaginous and soothing properties are used today in hi-tech dressings using calcium alginate *eg* carrageen, for non-stick dressings, which are easy to remove. According to oral folklore researched by the School of Scottish Studies[48] **Dulse**, **tangle** and other seaweeds, boiled with a little water and butter, have been used variously to treat constipation, to act as an appetite restorer and to put on boils or suppurating wounds to draw out pus.

Carrageen was used to make a stomach settler and a glutinous and soothing preparation for diarrhoea. A mixture of carragen and nettle was used for treating skin disorders including psoriasis.[48] **Sea Lettuce** and dulse were used as a cold compress for fevers, migraines, burns and cuts.

ALLIUM CEPA
ONION

Both the bulb and juices are used. Traditional uses include the treatment of hypertension, bronchial catarrh, typhoid and other infectious diseases. As the child of a highlander I was told that according to oral tradition a boiled onion placed under my armpit would draw out any poisons – a not unreasonable idea as the armpit has so many bloodvessels and glands.

We now know that onions contain flavonoids, which are anti-inflammatory.[12] The active principals of onions are sulphur compounds as in garlic.

ALLIUM SATIVUM
GARLIC

This was widely used medicinally by the Egyptians, who gave it to the workers who built the pyramids;[41] and by the Romans, who gave it to their soldiers to

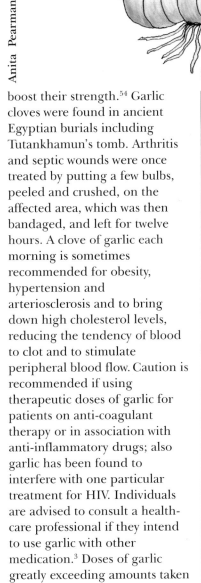

Anita Pearman

Garlic

boost their strength.[54] Garlic cloves were found in ancient Egyptian burials including Tutankhamun's tomb. Arthritis and septic wounds were once treated by putting a few bulbs, peeled and crushed, on the affected area, which was then bandaged, and left for twelve hours. A clove of garlic each morning is sometimes recommended for obesity, hypertension and arteriosclerosis and to bring down high cholesterol levels, reducing the tendency of blood to clot and to stimulate peripheral blood flow. Caution is recommended if using therapeutic doses of garlic for patients on anti-coagulant therapy or in association with anti-inflammatory drugs; also garlic has been found to interfere with one particular treatment for HIV. Individuals are advised to consult a health-care professional if they intend to use garlic with other medication.[3] Doses of garlic greatly exceeding amounts taken in food should not be taken during pregnancy as it was reputed to cause abortion. Garlic's many sulphur compounds are the reason for its notorious smell, and may be associated with its health benefits. Its odourless products, which are popularly sold, may not contain the active principals.[44] Garlic's anti-bacterial, anti-fungal, anti-viral and anti-parasitic properties should make it a valuable remedy for many common infections. Its efficacy as a drug has been researched and results reviewed by Barnes *et al*.[3]

ALOE VERA
ALOE VERA

This plant which is very popular in herbal medicine is grown only under glass in this country. A clear gel exuded from the mucilaginous tissue in the centre of the leaf is said to be a remarkably effective healer of wounds and burns, speeding up the rate of healing and reducing the risk of infection. This action is, in part, due to *aloectin B*, said to stimulate the immune system; however, further clinical studies are required to confirm this.[3] The protective and healing action is said to work internally and the gel has been used for peptic ulcers and irritable bowel syndrome.[7] The gel has been reported to be effective in the treatment of mouth ulcers.

ALOYSIA TRIPHYLLA
LEMON VERBENA

Fresh leaves were used as a tea in the treatment of nausea, indigestion, palpitations and vertigo. An infusion of dried flowers has been used as a mouthwash and purgative. Prolonged use may cause gastric irritation.[54] Individuals with existing liver damage should not use this.[3]

Anita Pearman

Lemon Verbena

ALTHAEA OFFICINALIS
MARSH-MALLOW

Official medical herbs often have *officinalis* as part of their Latin name. The ancient Egyptians used this as a soothing, healing herb, and prescribed it as a decoction for asthma. They made use mainly of the root. Around 370BC the herb was reportedly used in sweet wine for coughs: indeed it was used whenever a soothing effect was needed as it protected the mucous membranes. Its high mucilage content soothes irritation and inflammation of the alimentary canal such as inflammation of the mouth, pharynx, gastro-intestinal tract or peptic ulcers.[44] It was also used in treatment of urinary and respiratory organs.[24] Although no toxicity data have been reported, the chemistry of marsh-mallow and its use in

A Garden of Herbs

foods over a long period of time indicate that it is safe.[44] It may however interfere with hypoglycaemia (low blood sugar) therapy and affect the absorption of other drugs taken simultaneously.[3]

ANETHUM GRAVEOLENS
DILL

The ancient Egyptians classified dill as a soothing medicine. Biblical references show that it had a high enough value to be used for tax payments. Fragments were found at a Roman fort near Glasgow, although dill was found in Scotland before then.[14] The Saxon word 'della' means 'to lull'. It has long been taken for colic, wind, indigestion and constipation and as a tranquilliser. The seeds have a volatile oil which relaxes muscles and relieves spasm in the digestive tract.[34] Dill water, infused from the leaves, is excellent for flatulence in children. Gripe water, of which dill is a constituent, is still used for babies to induce sleep and cure hiccoughs.[5]

ANGELICA ARCHANGELICA
GARDEN ANGELICA

According to Harvey,[29] who made a study of the dates of arrival in Britain of many plants, it was known in Britain by 995AD and subsequently (all references to plants arriving by this date refer to Harvey). According to the Oxford Dictionary *Herba Angelica* the 'angelic herb' has reputed properties against poisons and pestilence. All parts of the plant are used and are

Marsh-mallow

said to stimulate appetite, and it has been tried in the treatment of anorexia nervosa. Tea made from the dried or fresh leaves has been used as a tonic for colds and to reduce flatulence. Its constituents are a volatile oil and derivatives of coumarins that stimulate digestion; however, herbs with coumarins should be used with caution because of potential interaction

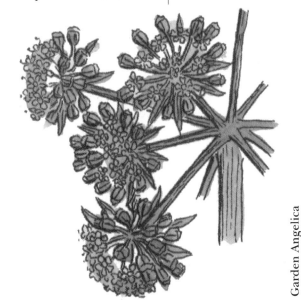

Garden Angelica

which their cattle were subject, especially that called the black disease'.* One of angelica's Gaelic names *cuinneog mhighe* means roughly 'the whey bucket' and is thought to be so-called because it was used to curdle milk. It was therefore not thought wise to let cows eat it.[34]

ANTHRISCUS CEREFOLIUM
GARDEN CHERVIL

A basket of chervil seeds was found in Tutankhamun's tomb, (died *c.*1350 BC), so it must have been considered an important herb. It was known in Britain by 995AD and subsequently. Fresh leaves are used to make warm poultices to apply to painful joints.[54] Juice from the fresh plant is used for skin conditions including wounds and eczema. The raw leaf can be used in salads for additional vitamin C, carotene, iron and magnesium. Infused as a tea it is believed to stimulate digestion and lower blood pressure.[12]

ARMORACIA RUSTICANA
HORSE-RADISH

It was used as a medicinal plant from the fourteenth century and as a relish from the sixteenth century.[34] It was said to stimulate the digestion, increasing gastric secretions though in large doses it may produce inflammation of the mucous membranes. It contains vitamin C and antibiotic substances. The sliced fresh root was used applied to inflamed joints and tissues, but horse-radish oil should not be used as it is one of the most hazardous of all essential oils and is not now recommended for external or internal use.

with anticoagulant therapy.[3] Angelica is supposedly of benefit in treating bronchitis and bronchial catarrh and also stimulates peripheral blood flow. It is considered by some to be a specific cure for a condition that narrows the arteries to hands and feet.[12] Angelica may provoke a photosensitive allergic reaction and large doses could interfere with anticoagulant therapy. The use of *bergapten* (present in angelica) in cosmetics or suntan preparations is stated to be ill-advised by some regulatory authorities, as there may be a risk of skin cancer.[3]

ANGELICA SYLVESTRIS
WILD ANGELICA

'The people of Assynt say that a decoction of the roots of angelica was very efficacious in removing some distempers to

Horse-radish should not be eaten to excess.[44]

ARTEMISIA ABROTANUM
SOUTHERNWOOD

This strongly smelling herb repels insects. It was known here by 995AD. As it is very bitter it was thought to strengthen digestive secretions in stomach and intestine, so it was used as an infusion to treat indigestion and intestinal problems. The dried plant used to be mixed with treacle to treat worms in children, but this is not recommended without professional supervision.

ARTEMISIA ABSINTHIUM
WORMWOOD; ABSINTHE

This plant is possibly native or, more probably, was introduced early as a medicinal herb. In Russia the plant's name is 'Chernobyl'.[39] The aerial parts contain several harmful substances, including a hallucinogen, so it produces some of the most dangerous alcoholic drinks. Absinthe wine, which also tends to become addictive, was banned in some countries but absinthe is considered a useful medical herb as it increases stomach and other digestive secretions and thus improves digestion and absorption of nutrients. It is safe in small doses but toxic in excess.[12] For kidney stones and urine retention an infusion of the plant in water taken two or three times a day was recommended. It was used in the sixteenth century to treat fleas; internal worms were traditionally treated, as the name suggests,[39] the powdered wormwood being added to white wine. The wine did nothing to the worms but it may have cheered up the patient.

Wormwood

ASPARAGUS OFFICINALIS
ASPARAGUS

It became an 'official' medicinal herb due to its laxative properties – perhaps because of its high fibre content. Some herbalists claim that it increases libido.[54]

BETULA
BIRCH

Birch oil, which is distilled from the bark, is astringent and is often used for its curative value in shampoos for skin infections, including eczema. The ash from birch mixed with butter or fat is said to be useful for ringworm.[5] Dried young leaves were formerly used to treat gout, rheumatism and dropsy.[24]

Borage

BORAGO OFFICINALIS
BORAGE

Dried flowering plants or fresh leaves are said to stimulate milk flow in nursing mothers. Borage is a mild diuretic, and was once used for kidney and bladder inflammation; also as a tisane for rheumatism and respiratory infections. With its high mucilage content it was used to sooth respiratory problems and helps sore and inflamed skin – prepared either as freshly squeezed juice in a poultice or as an infusion. The seed oil is even richer in polyunsaturated fats than evening primrose oil (EPO) (*see also* under Oenothera). Borage (starflower oil) and EPO were found to reduce systolic blood pressure and heart rate in cases of acute stress. Caution should be observed in use of borage oil and EPO in epileptic patients who are on phenothiazines. As borage has some toxic alkaloids prolonged ingestion is not recommended.[3]

BUXUS SEMPERVIRENS
BOX

A volatile oil from the wood was used to treat piles, and a decoction was used to treat secondary syphilis and other venereal diseases. Although animals in this country are said not to touch box, some animals have died from eating the leaves.[24]

CALAMINTHA OFFICINALIS
CALAMINT

This was an 'official' herb of the medical pharmacopoeia in medieval times, but is more often thought of as an ornamental aromatic plant by medical herbalists today, although it can be used as flavouring and seasoning. According to Culpeper's *The English Physician* (1653) it 'hinders conception' and 'works very violent upon the feminine part'. The active constituent is the same as in pennyroyal (*see Mentha pulegium*), so it is not safe to use if pregnant. It is said to stimulate sweating and hence lower fever, and to be useful for mild respiratory infections.[12]

CALENDULA OFFICINALIS
POT MARIGOLD

Marigold is one of the most useful herbs in Western medicine. Known here by 995AD and used continuously since, it is, above all, a remedy for most minor skin problems. Infusions and 'Calendula' the ointment, containing calendula extract, are mainly used to treat inflamed and angry skin, including minor burns, acne and some rashes and fungal conditions such as ringworm and athlete's foot. It is helpful for nappy rash and its antiseptic and healing properties help prevent the spread of infection and speed up repair. A tincture has been used to treat eczema. I, personally, have found marigold to be more efficacious in the treatment of psoriasis than conventional treatments, some of which include the use of steroids. Taken as an infusion, it is said to help inflammatory problems of the digestive system, and is also useful in treating stomach ulcers and colitis. It is also considered cleansing for the liver and gallbladder. [12] Animal studies have reported wound healing and anti-inflammatory effects, supporting some of the traditional uses of calendula in skin conditions. It may, however, cause allergic reactions in susceptible patients. Oral use is not recommended in pregnancy.[3]

CALLUNA VULGARIS
HEATHER
In the Highlands heather shoots or flowers were used as a poultice or in a pillow to give a refreshing sleep, after their use in bedding had died out.[5] Heather tea was also considered good for the 'nerves'. The combined action of the constituents of heather is predominantly antibacterial,[54] and it was thus used in the treatment of kidney and urinary tract infections and diarrhoea. It has been included in cleansing mixtures for acne. Extracts have long been used in homeopathic medicine in the treatment of bladder stones.[34]

CATHARANTHUS ROSEUS
MADAGASCAR PERIWINKLE
Vincristine and vinblastine are manufactured from this periwinkle (once considered a species of Vinca – hence the name of the drug) and are used as a chemotherapy treatment for cancer. Several of periwinkle's alkaloids were found to destroy white blood cells: vincristine and vinblastine are used to treat acute leukaemias, lymphomas and some solid tumours *eg* of breast and lung.*

Heather

CHAMAEMELUM NOBILE
ROMAN CHAMOMILE
MARTICARIA RECUTITA
SCENTED MAYWEED
GERMAN CHAMOMILE
These herbs are used in similar ways though the chemistry of German chamomile has been better documented. Chamomile oil is distilled from the flower heads. Aromatherapists use the oil to treat depression, headaches and insomnia. Chamomile tea, made by infusing flowers in boiling water and covering for ten minutes, has long been taken as an aid to

Studies have shown little toxicity, but care must be taken if on other medication for allergies or if on anticoagulant therapy, as they may interact.[3]

CHELIDONIUM MAJUS
GREATER CELANDINE

This plant, used medicinally since classical times, was formerly cultivated, and today grows near where people live. It is considered by Dickson & Dickson[14] to have been grown by monks in medieval times, when it was chiefly used to remove film from the cornea of the eye. It is recorded that it was used for this purpose in Scotland in 1767 (though noted in earlier herbals). It is not used for this purpose today. It was found at Paisley Abbey and in monastic deposits in Germany and Denmark (in the thirteenth and fifteenth centuries).[14] Fresh or dried flower were used for inflammation of the bile duct and gall-bladder and the fresh juice or latex is used externally on warts. It was used in homeopathy for jaundice. It has a very bitter taste and this

digestion, especially after heavy meals. Others say that combined with ginger it is good for indigestion, heartburn and colic when taken and hour before a meal. Flowers used in a bath are said to relieve sunburn. A wide range of pharmacological activities has been found in clinical studies. These include anti-inflammatory and wound-healing; an ointment preparation from chamomile was found to be as good as or superior to hydrocortisone in treatment of certain skin conditions and it has been found to be efficacious in healing weeping wounds associated with cutaneous leg wounds and haemorrhoids.[3] It has been applied to sore and itchy skin and eczema, but avoid it if you are allergic to other plants in the daisy family. Sedative effects have been documented. All these effects confirm many of the herbal usages. It is not recommended for babies.

A Garden of Herbs

stimulates the appetite and triggers the secretion of digestive juices, improving the digestive process. Large doses are poisonous.[44]

COCHLEARIA OFFICINALIS
SCURVY GRASS

The Gaelic name means the sailor. This fleshy-leaved plant grows near the sea and we know it was collected (perhaps as a growing plant) to take on long voyages as a cure for scurvy and noted as a treatment for this by Gerard (1597).[20] It was also cultivated, probably near the shore, as a useful vegetable providing the much-required vitamin C.

CORIANDRUM SATIVUM
CORIANDER

Coriander has been cultivated as a medicinal herb for at least 3,000 years. The Chinese believed it conferred immortality. It was brought to northern Europe by the Romans. In the Middle Ages it was put in love potions as an aphrodisiac. It is said that the seed can be chewed or infused as a tea, as an aperitif, a digestive tonic and a mild sedative. The bruised seeds can, it is said, be applied externally as a poultice for painful arthritic joints and they are used to prevent griping caused by other medication, such as senna, as the seeds are said to stimulate secretion of gastric juices.[54]

Hawthorn

CRATAEGUS MONOGYNA
HAWTHORN

Like rowan this was a magic plant of the Highlands,[48] where it was traditionally used as a decoction to cure sore throats and as an infusion for the control of blood pressure.[5] The parts used were the flowers and dried berries. The main use of hawthorn today is in the herbal industry (for other uses *see* Culinary section). Throughout the world nearly a thousand of its products are in use. Western herbalists consider it literally to be a 'food for the heart', increasing blood flow to the heart muscle. Today, products of hawthorn including flavonoids are mainly used in conventional medicine for heart and circulatory disorders, in particular for angina, coronary heart disease and high blood pressure, but hawthorn used in self treatment may affect existing treatment for heart problems so is not suitable for self-medication.[3] Combined with

Herbs & Medicine

ginkgo it is used by herbalists to enhance memory. Recent research has confirmed its cardiovascular actions.

COLCHICUM AUTUMNALE
AUTUMN CROCUS

The flower looks like a crocus but is really a lily. The whole plant is very poisonous and has always been a problem for grazing animals. It was used in the Middle Ages to treat gout and joint pains. Because it was so poisonous it ceased to be used until the nineteenth century when in 1822 one of its constituents *colchicine* was isolated and it began again to be considered one of the best remedies for gout. Today it is one of the treatments for leukaemia. The herb has significant side effects. As it affects cell division it can cause foetal abnormalities. It is subject to legal restrictions in some countries.[12]

Broom

CUMINUM CYMINUM
CUMIN

Formerly it was used to treat diarrhoea and dyspepsia. The seeds contain volatile oils and flavonoids * and have been used to relieve flatulence and to stimulate the digestive system. In Indian medicine cumin is used for insomnia and fevers.

CYNARA CARDUNCULUS
GLOBE ARTICHOKE

The leaf and root have been used for jaundice, liver insuffic-iency and anaemia and it was considered to be good for treat-ing gall-bladder problems. It is reported to be a stimulant to liver cell regeneration and action.[44] All parts of the plant stimulate the digestive system, especially production of bile, and it is a major constituent of some proprietary digestive tonics.[54] According to Chevallier, artichoke can be taken during early stages of late-onset diabetes, being a good food for diabetics as it significantly lowers blood sugar.[12] For possible allergic reactions to members of the daisy family see under *Achillea millifoleum*. Excessive use in pregnancy should be avoided. Clinical trial data are reviewed by Barnes *et al.*[3]

CYTISUS SCOPARIUS
BROOM

Several sources testify to the success of a decoction of broom as a remedy for dropsy. [5] Broom, however, contains toxic alkaloids, so is not suitable for self-medication.[44]

A Garden of Herbs

DAPHNE MEZEREUM
MEZEREON SPURGE OLIVE

This plant has been long grown in cottage gardens, for its wonderful fragrance in early spring. The root and bark were used in the treatment of venereal disease. It is exceedingly poisonous: only a few of the attractive fruits could kill a child.[34] The plant is now used only in homeopathy.

Spurge Olive

DAUCUS CAROTA
WILD CARROT

Poultices of wild carrot, and of cultivated varieties, were used in the Highlands to 'treat ulcerous or carcinogenic sores and used to sweeten the intolerable foetor of cancer' (Pennant, 1772). This seems a treatment worth further study. The whole plant smells of carrot. The cultivated carrot (the wild carrot root is spindly) was perhaps developed from subspecies *sativus*, probably brought to Britain in the fifteenth century.

DIGITALIS PURPUREA
FOXGLOVE

For thousands of years man has suffered from dropsy – a severe form of oedema. In Gaelic traditional medicine, and in parts of Europe, a concoction of foxgloves was used for some skin conditions and boils and as a remedy for dropsy due to heart disease,[5] which is still one of the most common causes of death and morbidity. The symptom of dropsy is now controlled by use of various diuretics. A link between dropsy and heart disease was not understood until William Withering went to study medicine in Edinburgh and met the distinguished botanist John Hope. He learned from Hope, that for centuries simple people had been treating dropsy with a mixture of herbs including foxglove leaves. Withering worked on this for many years looking at the effect on the heart and eventually gave us in 1785 one of the most significant breakthroughs in medical research.[34] Several glycosides including *digoxin* are extracted from the dried leaves of mainly *Digitalis lanata* (the woolly foxglove) and used to treat heart failure by causing the heart muscle to work more efficiently. This reduces the volume of blood accumulating in the heart chambers, therefore increasing circulation and allowing the kidneys to work more efficiently.[54] Foxglove is a very poisonous plant and not suitable for self medication.

Foxglove

Dryopteris filix-mas
Male Fern

Male Fern is highly toxic but dried rhizome and frond bases were used by the medical profession to get rid of tapeworms until early this century. The toxins act by paralysing the worm thus relaxing its hold on the gut wall. The medicine had to be taken with a non-oily purgative.

Echinacea angustifolia
Coneflower

Several species of Echinacea are used in herbal medicine. Commission E, the committee that judges the value of herbal medicine for the German government, has approved it as a treatment for 'flu-like' symptoms.[34] Modern herbalists claim that it stimulates a group of cells, known as macrophages, which 'eat' matter foreign to the body, stimulating the immune system in the body to give an increased resistance to infection.[40] Some of the claims for it include 'usefulness' in general infections, those in the mouth area and various skin diseases. Documented scientific evidence from animal studies supports some of its uses, including stimulation of the immune system. Further clinical studies using standardised preparations are required in order to verify this. It may interfere with immunosuppressive therapy, so if on any medication it should not be taken unless advised by a health professional.[44] Echinacea can be toxic to the liver and should not be combined with drugs that might cause liver damage.*

Viper's-bugloss

Echium vulgare
Viper's-bugloss

This bright blue flower is being trialled in north-east Scotland as a commercial crop; fields of it will look spectacular. An oil is produced by crushing the seeds. This oil contains gamma-linolenic acid and stearidonic acid, an omega-3 acid that is strongly anti-inflammatory and in demand for skin care. It can be used to treat burn victims. It is also used as an anti-wrinkle cream which which may offer a safer natural alternative to botox, so popular with Hollywood stars. Botox is a treatment involving injection of a toxin into the face to paralyse muscle and so smoothe out wrinkles, but it can produce permanent disfigurement.**

ERYNGIUM MARITIMUM
SEA-HOLLY

The fresh or dried root was used and was once considered to be of value in the treatment of genito-urinary irritation and infection, especially local inflammations of mucous membranes and of painful urination. Today it is said to be of use as a diuretic and for treating cystitis and kidney stones, but I have found no confirmation of its efficacy.

EUPATORIUM PERFOLIATUM
BONESET

The name boneset is a mystery as it does not appear ever to have been used for this purpose. It is native to North America and was used by native Americans to cure colds and fevers. The European settlers regarded it as a cure-all and its strange name is said to come from its ability to treat what was called 'break-bone fever'. This herb, as a hot infusion, was popularly used to treat influenza, acute bronchitis and congestion of the respiratory tract. It was as popular as hot lemon tea is today and probably more effective. It is emetic in large doses.[54] Boneset is a member of the daisy family and potentially allergic reactions may occur. It may stimulate the immune system as has been demonstrated in laboratory studies, supporting the traditional uses of the plant in influenza.[3]

EUPHORBIA HIRTA
ASTHMA WEED

As with all species of *Euphorbia* the latex that is exuded when the stems are bruised is an irritant to the skin; it can be applied externally, with care, in the treatment of warts.[54]

FILIPENDULA ULMARIA
MEADOWSWEET

More than a hundred pharmaceutical products containing meadowsweet are marketed. The plant was traditionally used for treating fevers and headaches in the Highlands and Islands.[5] Aspirin was first synthesised by the Bayer company in the 1880s from salicylic acid present in meadowsweet. The main uses are for alimentary tract disorders and rheumatism. Unlike aspirin, however, meadowsweet appears to be protective to the stomach lining while providing the anti-inflammatory benefit. There is documented scientific evidence for some of the antiseptic, anti-rheumatic and astringent actions, despite the absence of human clinical data.[3]

Meadowsweet

Fennel

GALANTHUS NIVALIS
SNOWDROP
This plant is native to Switzerland, but it may have been anciently native in Shropshire also; however it was not recorded as growing wild here until the 1770s.[39] It is a poisonous plant. Crushed bulbs were said to be suitable for application externally for frostbite.[54] The alkaloid *galanthamine*, present in snowdrop, is under test for the treatment of Alzheimer's disease. *

GALIUM ODORATUM
WOODRUFF
The dried plant was used for biliary obstruction and to treat varicose veins and phlebitis. Coumarin released from the dry plant is a source of modern anticoagulant drugs, confirming some of its former uses. Thus it should not be taken along with anticoagulant therapy.[3]

FOENICULUM VULGARE
FENNEL
The dried leaves, oil and dried ripe fruit are all used in medicine. The oil is included in purgatives to prevent griping. The leaves are calming to the stomach, prevent flatulence, and are mildly laxative. The seeds, combined with bearberry, are recommended as an excellent treatment for cystitis, and an infusion of the seeds is also used as a gargle for sore throats. Seeds are said also to be an aid to weight loss and to longevity; but too many seeds are toxic.[12]

FRAGARIA VESCA
WILD STRAWBERRY
The roots were formerly used to treat gonorrhoea. In Europe the fruit is considered to have diuretic properties and has been prescribed as part of a diet for arthritic people.

GAULTHERIA PROCUMBENS
FALSE WINTERGREEN
This American plant is commonly, but wrongly, called wintergreen. It was grown in Britain by 1762. The plant contains a useful oil called wintergreen, that is now mainly produced synthetically. An infusion of the leaves is used as a throat gargle and as a douche. It is strongly anti-inflammatory and antiseptic and said to be soothing to the digestive systems while being effective for arthritis, being the main ingredient of once popular Sloane's Liniment.[12] It should not be taken by people sensitive

to aspirin, and the oil should not be taken internally. It should not be applied (even well diluted) to children's skin unless under medical supervision.[12] Oil of wintergreen is today well known by athletes as it is commonly used before a race. It is rubbed into the skin over the muscle area to stimulate blood flow to the muscles; it is also used to relax strained muscles and before a important race many athletes smell of this!

GERANIUM MACULATUM
AMERICAN CRANE'S-BILL
The dried rhizomes were used in treatment of diarrhoea and haemorrhage of the gastrointest-inal tract; also in the treatment of haemorrhoids,[54] and often for irritable bowel syndrome.[12] The native *Geranium dissectum*, Cut-leaved Crane's-bill, has similar properties.[24]

GINKGO BILOBA
MAIDENHAIR TREE
Medicinal uses of ginkgo leaves were recorded by the Chinese in about 2800BC. There is some evidence to show that ginkgo preparations are effective in treating circulatory problems in the limbs and brain, and in treating asthma patients. There are also claims that ginkgo is beneficial in geriatric memory loss. All these claims are of considerable interest; recent clinical trials have been reviewed by Barnes *et al*,[3] and there is some supporting clinical evidence for its uses in dementia. Further clinical studies are underway. Contact with the fruit pulp has produced severe allergic reactions.

GLYCYRRHIZA GLABRA
LIQUORICE
Has been used medicinally for 3000 years and recorded on Egyptian papyri. Today it is one of the most popular and versatile herbal remedies. The root is used and preparations are demulcent, laxative and anti-inflammatory. It was used in the treatment of gastric ulcers and is of value for coughs and bronchitis. Until 1965 there was no drug available to assist in healing peptic ulcers; rest and a bland diet were the only forms of therapy. Two derivatives of liquorice were found to reduce the size of an ulcer very quickly and healing followed.[34] It should be eaten in moderation and avoided by people with heart disease, as large doses may lead to water retention, and hypertension. It may also interfere with hormonal treat-ment and in view of associated oestrogenic and other steroid effects it was traditionally report-ed to stimulate abortion, so it should be avoided in pregnancy.[44]

HAMAMELIS VIRGINIANA
VIRGINIAN WITCH HAZEL
Bark, leaves and flower-bearing twigs are used in an eye lotion and an ointment to treat haemorrhoids.[54] The leaves have astringent tannins which are used in suppositories.[34] Makes an excellent lotion for burns, inflammatory conditions of the skin, bruises, insect bites and varicose ulcers. Care must be taken not to confuse the lotion with the tincture made from the bark or leaves: this is extremely astringent and may cause disfigurement to the skin.[54]

Herbs & Medicine

stimulants, painkillers and sedatives. A pillow stuffed with hops is reputed to have cured George III's insomnia thus popularising this sleep-aid. Hop is also useful, combined with valerian, for insomnia, especially if the sleeplessness is associated with nervous tension. It should not be used by anyone suffering from depression, as it may react with prescribed drugs.[3]

HEDERA HELIX
IVY

Ivy was highly regarded as a magical plant protecting against evil spirits. The leaves were used and picked as required to make decoctions, ointments or tinctures etc. They were used, soaked in vinegar, as a medication for corns.[48] Ivy was used internally to treat gout and rheumatic pain, and as an anti-spasmodic in the treatment of whooping cough and bronchitis; it loosens and thins mucus from the tubes and lungs and helps troublesome coughs. As all parts are harmful if eaten it should be prescribed only by qualified practitioners.[7]

HUMULUS LUPULUS
HOP

Hops were used in medicine long before their use in flavouring beer. They were recognised as appetite

HYOSCYAMUS NIGER
HENBANE

Henbane has been used as a medicinal herb for thousands of years. An early Egyptian papyrus (c.1500BC) recorded it as being smoked to relieve toothache, and this use persisted throughout the Middle Ages. It reputedly produces the sensation of flying and is supposed to have been used by witches. Remains of henbane, or its pollen, have been found round old castles and abbeys.[14] The flowers contain a relatively high *hyoscyamine* content making extracts potentially toxic but giving it a more specifically sedative action than others of this very poisonous group of plants which includes deadly nightshade.* It is supposed to be very useful at controlling the pain of kidney stones, and its sedative affects have been used in treating the symptoms of Parkinson's disease. Henbane is mentioned again and again in old herbals.[29] It is used widely today in pre-operative medication and to prevent travel sickness and for other purposes. The capsules are toxic and only a few can be fatal to children. Henbane must not be self-administered.

A Garden of Herbs

HYPERICUM PERFORATUM
ST JOHN'S-WORT

Some accounts associate this herb with St John's Hospitallers, who looked after injured Crusaders, a forerunner of to-day's St John's Ambulance Service. Tradition tells that it was gathered on St John's Eve (23rd June) to be effective. St John's-wort is one of the oldest Highland cures, long considered very valuable. Tradition states that it was used by St Columba to treat a young boy whose nerves had been upset. The Gaelic name means 'The armpit package of St Columba' and tales relate how the Saint placed the herb under the boy's armpit and in time he was cured. Under the armpit was perhaps the most useful place known at that time for a poultice for herbs to be absorbed most successfully. [5]
In Europe, it is prescribed by general practitioners to treat depression. Short-term clinical trials indicate that it is as good as synthetic anti-depressants with fewer side effects. The only noted side effect is when pale-skinned people expose themselves to too much sunlight it increases photosensitivity. It is said to be an anti-inflammatory drug suited to treat auto-immune conditions like rheumatoid arthritis. Anti-viral activity has been reported against HIV and hepatitis, but recent work has not confirmed this. The major concern about using this herb is its ability to interact with some prescribed medicines including those used to treat transplant patients, heart conditions and blood clots, asthma, depression, migraine,

St John's-wort

HIV infection and oral contraceptives.[3] It appears to affect enzymes in the liver that may result in abnormally high or low levels of the drug in the body. * This herb must not be taken without consultation.

HYSSOPUS OFFICINALIS
HYSSOP
Pliny recommended hyssop as giving immunity to all diseases. It was known in Britain by 1200AD [29]. Today it is an under-valued medicinal herb but is still used for its mucilaginous properties, which soothe the digestive tract. It is said that hyssop oil can induce epileptic seizures, so it must only be used under professional supervision.[12]

IRIS PSEUDACORUS
YELLOW IRIS YELLOW FLAG
There is evidence that the rhizome was used since very early times as a purgative or to stop diarrhoea.[24] In the Highlands it was also used to treat toothache and inflamed throats.[5]

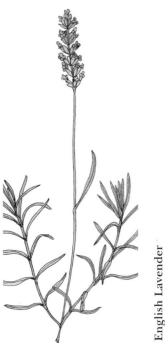

Anita Pearman

English Lavender

LAVANDULA ANGUSTIFOLIA
ENGLISH LAVENDER

Lavender has been used medicinally for centuries: embrocations were made from the oil to relieve pain and muscle stiffness, an infusuion of fresh leaves as a cold compress were given to relieve headaches and giddiness and the dried leaves in a herb cushion to encourage sleep. Flowers in an infusion were used as an antiseptic against acne; lavender water was regularly used as an antiseptic wash for wounds and as a fragrant wash to repel lice, flees, mosquitoes and other pests. The Romans had special lavender posy holders to deter bed-bugs. (*see* various lavenders in the Aromatic section)

LIGUSTICUM SCOTICUM
SCOTS LOVAGE

In Alistair Maclean's (1937) *Hebridean Altars** it is claimed that 'its soothing property gave quiet to the mind', being a reputed aphrodisiac like its close relative celery. It was one of the green vegetables given to people suffering from scurvy. Scots lovage makes an excellent cordial for a cold night, but should not be taken during pregnancy or by people with kidney problems. A broth made from lamb and lovage was given to people suffering from an uncertain condition known as *glaccach*, probably consumption, for which the nourishing broth may have been helpful. [5]

MALUS DOMESTICA
APPLE

The crab-apple is native to Britain but eating apples were always abundant in France and possibly were brought here by the Romans. Pliny mentioned twenty-two varieties so our ancestors must have known of them and of their medicinal value. A decoction of apples and rowan was used for whooping cough in the Highlands,[5] and in the *Regimen Sanitatis* the Beatons recommended cleaning the teeth with apple skins, and taking a roasted apple to help sleep and before heavy meals to aid digestion.[2] This advice was given to me as a child by my Highland father confirming the value of oral tradition.

Scots Lovage

A Garden of Herbs

MALVA SYLVESTRIS
COMMON MALLOW

Quantities of mallow pollen were found at the Roman fort near Glasgow where the seeds, leaves and flowers were all eaten by the Romans, both as food and as a kind of preventative medicine.[14] Pliny said that a daily dose would make you immune to all diseases. It is still used for its mucilaginous properties to soothe gut irritations and it has a laxative effect.[7]

MANDRAGORA OFFICINARUM
MANDRAKE

This plant, especially the berries, is very poisonous, containing *scopolamine*, long known to be hallucinogenic. According to Celsus, the Roman medical historian, a concoction with opium, henbane and wine or vinegar was known as 'the death wine' being offered on a sponge to prisoners about to be crucified. They fell into a death-like sleep, sometimes recovered when they were removed from the cross as dead. A fifth century manuscript recommends that it be given to induce sleep prior to an amputation. 'Let him drink an ounce and a half. . . he will sleep until the limb is removed.' It was regularly employed as a narcotic and anaesthetic until the fifteenth century. In 1900 it was used to produce 'twilight sleep' in obstetrics.*

MELISSA OFFICINALIS
LEMON BALM

This herb was known in Britain by 995AD.[29] A delightful tea made from the fresh leaves was originally drunk to help anxiety or depression and has long been used to calm the nerves. Today it is taken for nervous disorders, depression, anxiety and nervous headaches. Scholars used to drink the tea believing it sharpened the memory. It is being tested as an anti-agitation herb for people with Alzheimer's and results are encouraging.**

MENTHA
MINT

Mentha piperata **Peppermint**
This contains the oil menthol used as a local analgesic for sprains and bruises and as an antiseptic, also for toothache and colds. The leaf is infused as a tea to treat flatulence and relieve spasmodic pains of stomach and bowel.[34]
Mentha pulegium **Pennyroyal**
This is sedative, antispasmodic and a powerful purgative. It was used until about sixty years ago by 'back-street' abortionists, not very successfully, but often caused much trouble.*** (*see also* Culinary section)
Mentha spicata **Spearmint** The leaves are thought to be a cure for athlete's foot. Some people

Common Mallow

Herbs & Medicine

mix primrose leaves with mint to make a refreshing drink for flu and colds. One of the mints was used with castor oil to treat rheumatism in the Highlands.[48]

MENYANTHES TRIFOLIATA
BOG-BEAN

The name comes from a Greek word *menanthos* which means 'flower of the moon' (or month), perhaps reflecting its beneficial effect on menstrual pain, but I have found no recent herbal uses relating to women's problems. In the Highlands it has been taken for stomach upsets and ulcers and is still used in places.[5] In Shetland medicine it is also used as a sedative when boiled with peppermint and valerian, and with mint and raspberries it was used to treat gall-bladder problems.[48] Its greatest benefit is said to be as a tonic, stimulating gastric and bile secretions, hence promoting appetite, however according to recent work large doses may irritate the stomach and cause vomiting and diarrhoea,[3] but this research only relates to extracts from the leaf, and the root has long been used.

MYRICA GALE
BOG-MYRTLE

Aromatic resins from the leaves have been used to produce an insect repellent. On the Isle of Skye, in 1995, a commercial midge-repellent gel was marketed as Myrica. Trials have vindicated the plant's folk reputation.[39] An infusion was used to treat worms in children.[48] Gale beer is a traditional drink made from bog-myrtle which is often added to home-brew at early stages in beer-making.

OENOTHERA BIENNIS
EVENING-PRIMROSE

The seed oil has been used extensively as a food supplement for many years. It contains *linoleic* and *gamolenic* acids. Barnes *et al*[3] have reviewed much of the current research reported below. Clinical studies using evening primrose oil (EPO) in treatment of pre-menstrual syndrome have reported 'no beneficial effects' to 'marked improvement'. The results of treatment on multiple sclerosis are so far contradictory, although there may be some beneficial effect on the progress of the disease. *Linoleic* and *gamolenic* acids are effective in improvement, and reduction of associated itching, in moderate to severe eczema, and require-ment of steriods and anti-biotics is reduced. There is significant improvement in cerebral func-tion in Alzheimer's disease and delayed memory loss and schizophrenia symptoms with EPO. There was no significant behavioural improvement in one trial with EPO on hyperactive children. There was a significant effect on viral infection and post viral fatigue with EPO. Human studies are ongoing to assess the impact of gamolenic acid in various human cancers; animal studies show an inhibitory effect on tumour growth. There seem to be few side effects. It is reported to be non-toxic. Both acids are present in breast milk so it seems to be reasonable to assume it is safe to take when breast-feeding.*

A Garden of Herbs

Origanum vulgare
WILD MARJORAM; OREGANO
This species has an ancient medical reputation. The Greeks used it as hot fomentations to treat painful swellings and rheumatism. Internally it was a remedy for narcotic poisonings, convulsions and dropsy. It was also used to settle flatulence and to stimulate the flow of bile. Oregano contains a strongly antiseptic essential oil that was used to treat respiratory conditions such as coughs, bronchitis and asthma. The diluted oil is said to alleviate toothache and to soothe painful joints but must be used sparingly as it may cause skin irritation. A mixture of oregano and basil, stewed together and used as a poultice for mosquito bites is 'most efficacious'.[48] An infusion of the fresh plant will relieve nervous headaches by virtue of the camphoraceous substances in the oil.[24]

Origanum onites
POT MARJORAM
Large quantities of this are gathered in a cottage industry in the south of England and hung up to dry for making into marjoram tea that is said to help settle the nervous system and relieve anxiety, headaches and insomnia.[24]

Ocimum basillicum
BASIL
An infusion of fresh leaves is a mild laxative, good also for travel and morning sickness. Basil stimulates the appetite. (*see* Culinary section)

Evening-primrose

Panax ginseng, Panax quinquefolius & Panax pseudoginseng
GINSENG
The virtues claimed for this herb were too fantastic to be readily credited by Western medicine. Panax ginseng comes from China, Korea, Japan and Manchuria – the traditional source of the best ginseng. (When I was walking on the mountains of the Korea/China border a trader sold me a whole ginseng root for a very modest sum of money. It tasted and looked a bit like parsnip.) The other species grow wild in Canada and the USA and were used by indigenous people there.[10] Ginseng should be used with appropriate regard to traditional guidelines in countries where it has been used for centuries, and where it has been renowned for its ability to help the body build up resistance to diseases and strain, either physical or nervous.[54] It is

Common Poppy

interfere with the workings of some prescribed medicines, *eg* cardiovascular drugs, and that it could increase blood pressure if taken with caffeine.[44] There is some concern also about side effects, and so it is recommended that anyone on medication should consult a doctor before using this drug.

Papaver rhoeas
Common Poppy

A syrup of poppy flowers was used in Scotland as a mild soporific/narcotic. According to Cameron's *Gaelic Names of Plants* (1900) the juice of the red poppy was put into children's food in order to help them to sleep but it could become addictive. In South Uist, the flowers were an ingredient in a liquid teething mixture for toddlers.[5]

Papaver somniferum
Opium Poppy

The name *somniferum* means sleep-inducing. To the people believing in the doctrine of Signatures, the seed head resembled the human brain so should be used to soothe the brain.[38] All parts except the seeds are dangerous. Taken only under medical supervision, it provides the greatest of all painkillers, opium and morphine, which come from the unripe capsules of the poppy and have been used in medicine since earliest times. Opium contains many alkaloids, the major one being morphine.* Another important drug that is obtained from morphine is codeine (which also can be addictive). The seeds of this poppy grown here are safe to use.

said to stimulate and also to depress the central nervous system and improve hormone function. The 'tonic' properties of ginseng were confirmed in a study in 1967 that stated that doses taken over a long period resulted in improved well-being which lasted long after medication was stopped.[44] Research has shown pharmacological activities on the hypothalamic and pituitary regions of the brain.[54] Ginseng is considered to be a prime stimulant for the immune system by increasing the number of macrophages, thus helping the body to deal with infections. This view has been supported by extensive research.[3] A study to find out whether ginseng has something to offer our ageing society would be valuable. Statistical analysis of some of the work that has already been carried out in China into the effects of ageing may prove interesting. Recent research has indicated that ginseng may

A Garden of Herbs

PERSICARIA BISTORTA
BISTORT
The root has an acid taste and was used as a powerful astringent. The plant was allegedly very good for treating urinary complaints. Recommended by the Beatons* as a diet food for summer time, the leaves were used in salads.[2]

PETROSELINUM CRISPUM
PARSLEY
Parsley has long been an esteemed plant and was used to crown victors at important Roman games, and Homer relates that chariot horses were fed on its leaves. The fresh leaves are highly nutritious and are a natural vitamin and mineral supplement. The seeds have a strong diuretic effect and both seeds and leaves can be used in the treatment of gout and arthritis as they encourage the flushing out of waste products from the inflamed joints, eliminating them via the kidneys.[12] Parsley in medicinal quantities is phototoxic* and may increase the action of certain antidepressants and an irritant present in parsley oil may aggravate existing liver damage and may even act to abort a foetus in pregnant women, if taken in much larger quantities than in any normal culinary use.[3]

POTENTILLA ERECTA
TORMENTIL
In the Western Isles the root, really a rhizome, was boiled in milk to cure diarrhoea, chewed to heal sore lips, and also much used in the treatment of cholera,

while in Perthshire it was used in a lotion for sunburn.[48] The roots were used for many purposes, including tanning and dyeing, and on the islands of Tiree and Coll overuse led to a ban on digging it up, (possibly in the late nineteenth century) thus destroying the machair.[13] The name Potentilla means 'little powerful one' and it was once an official medical herb. All parts are strongly astringent, the rhizome especially so, and are used in treatment of diarrhoea and dysentery and make a beneficial gargle for throat infections, mouth ulcers and inflamed gums.[24]

Tormentil

PRUNELLA VULGARIS
SELFHEAL
On the island of Colonsay, selfheal was 'a popular remedy for chest ailments, it was collected in summer, tied in bundles, and hung up to the kitchen roof to dry for winter use. The plants were boiled in milk and strained before using; butter was added'. [McNeill, 1910 in *Vickery* [57]] It was also used by the common people, in Lightfoot's time (eighteenth century), 'as a vulnerary, bruised and applied to fresh wounds, drunk in broth in cases of internal bleeding or else injected for 'treating' the bloody flux [dysentery]'.[32] There used to be great faith in the plant as it was believed to remove all 'obstructions' from the liver, kidneys and spleen.[5] The herb has a long history as a wound healer and as a general tonic. The flowers are used in Chinese herbal medicine: unusually, however, the uses in China are

Selfheal

different from traditional European applications as it was used for fevers and 'liver weaknesses' (as in traditional Scottish uses). It is little used today but might be worth further investigation.

PRUNUS PADUS
BIRD CHERRY

PRUNUS AVIUM
GEAN WILD CHERRY

The pedicels (stalks of the flowers and fruits) were used to make an infusion or decoction with astringent properties for the treatment of bronchitis, anaemia and diarrhoea, and the gum from gean was dissolved in wine and used as a treatment for colds.[13] The fruit of gean containing *keracyanin* success-fully maintained normal uric acid levels in gouty patients before the introduction of the drug *colchicine* derived from meadow saffron, *Colchicum autumnale*.[34] Gout is now controll-ed by allozurinol, inhibitor of *xanthine oxidase*. Gout is caused by a build-up of uric acid crystals in the joints and *allozurinol* prevents these from forming.

PULMONARIA OFFICINALIS
LUNGWORT

Known in Britain by the sixteenth century. Faith in the Doctrine of Signatures suggested that because the markings on the leaves were thought to be reminiscent of the lung it should be used to cure lung disease.[38] Its high mucilage content does make it a useful remedy for chest conditions.[7] It is still used in ointments in the Highlands.[5]

PULSATILLA VULGARIS
PASQUE FLOWER

This is a poisonous herb although it is still in use. The dried aerial parts of the plant were used as a sedative and analgesic for headaches, earache and for menstrual pain. It is used in homoeopathy to treat measles. In France it is used traditionally to treat coughs and as a sedative to induce sleep.[3]

RANUNCULUS FICARIA
LESSER CELANDINE PILEWORT

The tubers are shaped like small, fleshy growths which may have suggested to people in the later Middle Ages that, according to the Doctrine of Signatures, they should be used to treat growths and piles.[38] The juice was applied externally to the part affected. Unfortunately the juice causes sores and blisters, so had to be applied with care.[5]

RHEUM X HYBRIDUM
RHUBARB

Rhubarb was originally imported from Russia because its root was used to treat constipation, once very common, perhaps because people did not eat many vegetables or fruit. An attempt was made to bring the root over the silk route from China. This failed as it perished on the way. Two different Scottish doctors who worked at the Russian Court, noted how important a treatment it was there, so brought or sent seed in 1723 and again in 1762 to the famous botanist John Hope (*see* Foxglove, page 33) when it was grown successfully in the Old Physic Garden in Edinburgh. It was also known to stimulate the gastric juices. At this time only the root was used. Its laxative action is well recognised today but non-standard products should not be used as results can be unpredictable.[44] People with inflammatory colon disease should not take the root medicinally. Long-term use should be avoided because it could interfere with cardiac drugs.[3] The leaves are very toxic.

Raspberry

RUBUS IDAEUS
RASPBERRY

The wild form of raspberry is a Scottish native plant, so cultivated varieties do well here where the climate suits them. According to Mary Beith,[5] boiled wild raspberries, flavoured with mint and bog-bean, were given to a patient after a bout of jaundice with success. In the Highlands, raspberry leaves used to be drunk in a tea by expectant mothers, as it was thought to strengthen the muscles of the womb. This use is said to be still widespread today in the Highlands,[5] a cause for concern as recent work has indicated that it may initiate uterine contractions so should not be taken during pregnancy.[3] Work has been carried out in Oregon State University into the vitamin and flavonoid content in raspberries. The study focuses on the high levels of ellagic acid – a rich food source in the fruit.

Clinical trials in USA are underway into the possible role of raspberries in prevention of some cancers, including cervical cancer.* A recent study of flavonoids in fruit, including raspberries, at Glasgow University, shows that these act as anti-oxidants and are anti-inflammatory in many test systems. Flavonoids are being investigated as potentially providing protection against cancer and heart disease.**

SALIX
WILLOWS
Aspirin-like compounds are found in willow bark, especially the purple willow. People used to chew the bark for pain relief. Aspirin has been made synthetically since 1899.

SALVIA OFFICINALIS
SAGE
An infusion of the leaves was used as a general tonic and to help cure coughs, colds, fevers and minor ailments. It was traditionally said also to aid digestion and to treat diarrhoea, and to be excellent for hot flushes associated with the menopause.[40] There is current research into the use of salvia in Alzheimer's disease.[3]

SALVIA VERBENACAEA
WILD CLARY
Wild clary is not unlike cultivated sage but is less aromatic. It is planted in churchyards – perhaps to confer immortality or to promote good health to the living. The name salvia comes from *salus* which means health, and clary means 'clear eye'. Its seeds were soaked in water and the resulting mucilage was once put on the eyes to soothe them.[39]

SAMBUCUS NIGRA
ELDER
Elder-flower leaves were crushed into an ointment for wounds and burns; the flowers, together with their pollen, were made into an ointment with almond oil to treat skin conditions where the skin was unbroken. Elderberry tea or wine was considered one of the best remedies for colds, flu and chest complaints like asthma and bronchitis.[5] It was traditionally used for its diuretic, laxative and local anti-inflammatory effects. These effects have been found in animal studies thus partially vindicating the traditional uses of elder. No clinical trials have been documented for elder. Poisonous substances have been found in the bark, leaves and unripe berries, so only the flowers and ripe fruits should be used in herbal remedies.[3]

A Garden of Herbs

SAPONARIA OFFICINALIS
SOAPWART
This was used traditionally for washing woollen fabric as its name suggests. A decoction of the root makes a soothing wash for itchy skin conditions. It has been prescribed for bronchitis, coughs and asthma,[12] but as soapwart is potentially toxic it should be used with care.

SATUREJA MONTANA &HORTENSIS
WINTER & SUMMER SAVORY
Savory was considered an antiseptic herb, beneficial to the digestive tract.[12] It was at one time in demand as an aphrodisiac.[54] It is deduced from remains, found at the Roman fort in Glasgow, that summer savory was used there as a green herb.[14] Savory's essential oil should not be used internally without professional supervision, especially during pregnancy.'[12]

SILYBUM MARIANUM
MILK THISTLE
This thistle is a Mediterranean species, introduced as a medicinal herb before the sixteenth century. According to the Doctrine of Signatures, the network of white veins on the leaves suggested it should be used to increase the supply of milk to lactating women and it was considered a suitable diet for wet nurses.[38] It is used as a bitter tonic, stimulating secretions of the stomach, intestine and gallbladder and it contains a mixture of substances reported to be protective against liver damage. The chemistry has been well documented and available data support many of the herbal uses, particularly in treatment of various liver disorders and there is evidence that it is safe in recommended doses in the short term.[3] People should always consult a health-care professional before using this drug. Milk thistle may cause allergic reactions in people sensitive to the daisy family. The safety of this drug has not been definitely established and there is a lack of toxicity data, so excessive use during pregnancy and lactation should be avoided.[3]

Milk Thistle

SPHAGNUM
BOGMOSSES
These were used for wound dressing and were collected for this during the two World Wars. They grow in and produce an acid environment, which does not allow bacteria to thrive, so are more than merely absorbent. They were used in some countries for babies' nappies and were collected to wipe down newly born infants.

STACHYS PALUSTRIS
MARSH WOUNDWORT

Woundwort has antiseptic properties and the leafy plant is said to have been used as a wound dressing, probably along with the highly absorbent sphagnum mosses, to staunch wounds on Scottish battlefields over one thousand years ago.[14]

STACHYS OFFICINALIS
BETONY

Betony was one of the great 'all healers' of the medical herbalists from classical times onwards. It was one of the main remedies for 'maladies of the head', and its properties as a tonic for nerves is still acknowledged. So many extravagant uses grew up around betony that later it was neglected, but strangely its leaves were used as a cough mixture: ironically it has also been used as a tobacco substitute. It was said that wild animals would seek out and eat betony if wounded and would be cured.[24] According to Beith[5] the uses of betony and germander speedwell may have been confused as their early names were similar, so the betony referred to in Highland remedies may actually be germander speedwell.

SYMPHYTUM OFFICINALE & TUBEROSUM
COMMON & TUBEROUS COMFREY; BONE-SET

The name comfrey is probably a corruption of the Latin *confervere* which means 'to grow together'. All the comfreys contain *allantoin* which promotes healing of connective tissue. Medieval herbalists called it bone-set. The roots were dug up in the spring and grated and the mucilaginous mass used as Plaster of Paris is today. Comfrey leaves can be used as a poultice for rough skin, aching joints, sores and burns and sprains to reduce swelling. In the form of an ointment comfrey was used for bites, stings and heat rash. Comfrey should not be applied where there is broken skin, nor should it be left in contact with the skin for a long period. Tea made from leaves and roots is said to relieve stomach ulcers, but comfrey should not be taken internally as it contains alkaloids that have been shown to cause liver damage and tumours in laboratory animals. Comfrey in the form of tablets or capsules (made from roots or leaves) is banned is several countries.[7]

A Garden of Herbs

TANACETUM PARTHENIUM
FEVERFEW

Feverfew derives its name from its ability to bring down fevers and was used to treat migraine headaches. It was the medieval world's 'aspirin'.[39] It has had its reputation vindicated by recent work at the City of London Migraine Clinic. A 70% decrease in frequency and severity of attacks has been reported.[39] The active chemicals in the leaves have been isolated and they stop blood vessels in the head going into spasm, which is believed to be the cause of migraine attacks. Taken as fresh leaves in bread and butter it has been used as an anti-inflammatory in cases of arthritis. Avoid feverfew if subject to mouth ulcers.[40] Dried flowers were once used in home remedies in Europe to induce abortion and to promote menstruation, so use with care.[34] People with a known sensitivity to the daisy family, especially if they develop a contact rash, should avoid its use.

TANACETUM VULGARE
TANSY

The whole plant is very bitter and aromatic. It has been much used in medicine and also in domestic economy as an ingredient of puddings. In Scotland, an infusion of the dried flowers and seeds (half to one teaspoonful two or three times a day), was given for gout. The roots, when preserved in honey or sugar have also been reputed to be of special service in treating gout, if eaten after fasting, every day for several days. Tansy was sometimes

Feverfew

Tansy

infused in whisky (or whey) as a treatment for worms. It was used also in much the same way as chamomile is today. Infused in hot water, it was thought to produce a calming drink – particularly for young children in the throes of a tantrum and anyone suffering from hysterics.[24] A potent cure for urinary complaints was made from tansy flowers, boiled and reduced down. One teaspoon was taken each day. Tansy was also used to treat scabies and was said to promote restful sleep. A glass of tansy wine is said to be good for insomnia; however, note that tansy in large doses is toxic.[44]

TARAXACUM OFFICINALE
DANDELION

Children were often told not to smell dandelions as this was thought to induce bed-wetting. The leaves are high in vitamins A and C, niacin and various minerals. The root increases bile production and is an effective diuretic. It is also considered to be good for rheumatism, constipation and insomnia.[44] Dandelion is reputedly an excellent internal cleansing agent, being one of the most effective detoxifying herbs. Excessive use of dandelion over what would normally be used in foods should be avoided. It may cause allergic reactions in individuals sensitive to members of the daisy family. Anyone with a liver complaint should first consult a health-care practitioner or doctor before using dandelion extracts.[40]

THYMUS
THYMES

The volatile oils of thyme, such as thymol, are phenols which are highly antiseptic, supporting the immune system in the fight against infections, particularly respiratory, digestive and genito-urinary systems.[7] They can act on the lungs, relaxing bronchial spasm and making mucus less cohesive. This helps the lung expel mucus so benefits bronchitis and chesty catarrhal symptoms.[40] Thyme was once carried in Judge's Posies and in the Sovereign's Maundy Thursday Posy; intended to protect against infectious diseases of the poor.[24] The posies in the children's rhyming game 'Ring a ring of roses' probably refer to similar protection against plague.

TUSSILAGO FARFARA
COLT'S-FOOT

The majority of the uses of colt's-foot are associated with its mucilage content. It is stated to have been used to treat intestinal problems and to alleviate bronchitis and catarrh. However it contains some toxic substances in low concentration so regular or excessive use of colt's-foot even in herbal teas should be avoided. It also could interfere with therapies for high blood pressure or heart disease.[44] It should not be taken in pregnancy.

URTICA DIOICA
COMMON NETTLE

Nettles have been used as food since prehistoric times. The Romans certainly ate nettles and may have used them to 'warm away' inflammations (perhaps to treat arthritis).[39] In the Highlands it was an important part of the spring diet, perhaps because of the lack of vitamin C in the winter. Nettle was considered a blood purifier,[48] and doctors advised families to eat nettle broth in March.[4] Today it is used by herbalists for allergic rashes and detoxification; its diuretic action is considered good for arthritis and gout. It should be avoided if you have diabetes or high blood pressure.[44] Nettle is widely used in Latin America for treating arthritis. When I was in Colombia, I underwent treatment necessitating that I should be stung all over the affected area. I cannot definitely say that it helped my arthritis but it certainly took my mind off it! I do know it is very much esteemed as a treatment in South America. This treatment was also part of our own herbal tradition, in which the affected joint was stung liberally; the joint being then moved gently for some little time after the application. It is said that relief was felt in thirty minutes or so, with a gentle tingling going on for some time. The treatment had to be repeated over a few days. 'Threshing' the body for rheumatism was still used on the island of Islay until recently.[48] This kind of treatment is to some extent similar to the modern use of bee venom for inflamed joints.[39] Nettle is also reputed to act as an abortifacient and to affect the menstrual cycle so should be avoided in pregnancy.[44]

Cranberry

VACCINIUM OXYCOCCUS CRANBERRY

VACCINIUM MACROCARPON LARGE CRANBERRY

The large cranberry is the species grown for commercial purposes today. The other is the Scottish wild cranberry. They are used commonly as foods, and have been used in the treatment of urinary tract infections. To date clinical studies do not provide compelling evidence of their efficacy in prevention of urinary tract infections, however results suggest that this area warrants further investigation. Some cranberry juice is high in sugar (dextrose and fructose) content. People using this juice to treat urinary tract infection should drink sufficient fluids in order to maintain adequate urine flow and should consult a health care professional for advice. Doses greatly exceeding normal use should not be taken during pregnancy.[3]

VACCINIUM MYRTILLUS
BLAEBERRY; BILBERRY

This was a valued healing herb in the Highlands.[5] It contains a group of flavonoids, which appear to have the ability to increase the rate of reproduction of visual pigments in the retina. The fruit, which is also nutritious, is recommended as a tonic for the eyes. Clinical trials (not all well designed) have investigated its effectiveness in ophthalmology and for improvements in microcirculation. It is too soon to make positive recommendations as to its usefulness.* [3]

VALERIANA OFFICINALIS
COMMON VALERIAN

Gerard[20] tells us that herbalists of his time thought it 'excellent for those burdened and for such as be troubled with croup and other like convulsions, and also for those that are bruised with falls'. He related that the dried root was held in such esteem as a medicine among the poorer classes in the northern counties and the south of Scotland, and that 'no broth or pottage or physical meats be worth anything if Setewale (the old name for Valerian) be not there'. Traditional use as a sedative and hypnotic has been supported by documented studies.[44] Valerian has been widely used to ease pain, nervous unrest, migraine, neuralgia and insomnia. It is said to be as effective as common tranquillisers, without being addictive.[53] Valerian is reputed to have been Hitler's favourite tranquilliser; it was also widely used as a tincture to treat soldiers suffering from shell shock. It is now known that the roots have quite strong sedative properties and an extract is found in many herbal tranquillisers. The tranquillising action has been attributed to constituents of the volatile oil that inhibit a chemical transmitter in the brain, helping to decrease activity in the nervous system and thus promoting sleep. Research on human subjects has indicated its effectiveness in moderating sleep disturbances.[3] It has been recommended as an alternative to orthodox sedatives, also in association with hops.[44] Valerian, however should not be taken along with other sedatives, nor should it be taken in large quantities over a long period.[54]

VERBENA OFFICINALIS
VERVAIN; VERBENA

This was once a venerated and magic plant and thought to be a cure for the plague. The church exorcised its magic by 'appropriating it' and suggesting that it grew under the cross! It has been prized as a tonic to help nervous tension and thought to have a mild antidepressant action and to assist in convalescence after fevers.[12] There is, however, still only limited chemical, pharmacological and toxicity data and documented scientific information does not justify its herbal uses. Excessive doses may interfere with hormone therapies and are said to act as an abortifacient or may affect lactation. Caution is advised if considering using vervain, especially during pregnancy. Its effect on lactation has been demonstrated by tests on animals.[44]

VINCA MAJOR & V. MINOR
PERIWINKLE &
LESSER PERIWINKLE
Both are sources of an alkaloid used in the pharmaceutical industry as a cerebral stimulant and vasodilator. Periwinkle helps to reduce high blood pressure. It should not be self-administered.

Notes

Page 15* Ghalioungui, P (1983) *The Physicians of Pharonic Egypt* Verlag, Phillip von Zabern

Page 15** Lazenby, E (1995) *Mandrake* The Scottish Society of the History of Medicine 1995-96

Page 15*** Spoer, HH (1907) *The Powers of Evil in Jerusalem*

Page 17* Pliny *Naturalis Historea* Hedge mustard Veda, Vol. 22.158 and Betony Vettonica, Vol. 25.84

Page 20* The Beatons, some of whose writings are in manuscript *Regimen Sanitatis* (Rule of Health), dating from *c.*1563 (National Library of Scotland), translated from the Gaelic, edited and published 1911, were an influential medical dynasty in the Highlands of Sotland.

Page 26* from James Robertson's *Tour of the Highlands 1767-71*

Page 29* British National Formulary

Page 32* Crozier, A *et al* (1997) *J. Agric. Food Chem.* 45 Flavonoids act as antioxidants and are anti-inflammatory in many test systems and are currently being investigated as potentially providing protection against cancer and heart disease.

Page 34* Barnes, J in *Risk of Drug and Herb Blend* reported by Woodham, A *The Times* 5th March 2002

Page 34** Pers. com. Booth, E Scottish Agricultural College *Press & Journal* 24th August 2002

Page 36* British National Formulary

Page 38* Henbane, deadly nightshade, mandrake and tomato are members of the same family as potato which has very poisonous shiny green fruits which look like unripe tomatoes.

Page 39* Barnes *et al* (2001) St John's-wort (a review of its chemistry, pharmacology and clinical properties) *Journal of Pharmacy and Pharmacology* Vol. 53 London

Page 40* Maclean, A. (1937) *Hebridean Altars: Some studies of the Spirit of an Island Race* Morey Press, Edinburgh

Page 41* Plants such as mandrake, belladonna, henbane contain *hyoscyamine* that can be changed into *atropine* – both very poisonous. In 1888 when mandrake was chemically analysed it was again recommended as a general and a local anaesthetic. Today it may be of value in treating people suffering from nerve gas inhalation. Lazenby, E (1995)

Mandrake The Scottish Society of the History of Medicine 1995-96

Page 41** Medical Research Centre, Newcastle: Cognative Neuro-Science Unit, Northumberland University.

Page 41*** Gibson, JA pers. com. Until about sixty years ago pennyroyal was commonly used by 'back street' abortionists, because it was a strong purgative. The 1941 Pharmacy and Medical Act forbade any information on uses of pennyroyal (also tansy and rue) to be made available, as so many attempted abortions ended in trouble. It was noted as early as 1683 in *Pharmacopoeia Edinburgensis Pauperum* that pennyroyal caused abortion

Page42* In the Wellness Guide to Dietary Supplements (www.berkeleywellness.com/html/ds/dsEveningPrimrose.php) it is reported that 'the body produces its own linoleic and gamolenic acids and that they are plentiful in foods taken in a normal diet; also that as primrose oil is very expensive and may oxidise if kept too long. This has influenced people to turn to borage oil which may contain liver toxins.' Some of these opinions require to be investigated.

Page 44* A white juice is obtained from unripe capsules – this is opium. It contains many alkaloids of which morphine is one. Codeine can be made commercially from this.

Page 45* Parsley, taken in excess, is phototoxic and contains substances that are activated by sunlight to produce skin reactions.

Page 48* Rommel, A & Wrolstad, RE (1993) *American J. Agric. & Food Chem.* 41

Page 48** There is recent research into the potential uses of flavonoids (present in raspberries) and other chemicals such as pyrrolizidines (which may cause liver damage), that are present in other plants. (*see* Page 32* above)

Page 54* Review article Morazzoni P, Bombardelli E, 1996 Vaccinium myrtillus L. Fitoterapia 66

Principle books or articles consulted

Newall *et al*[44] and Barnes *et al*[3] most recent pharmaceutical matters;

Beith[5] Scottish/Highland history of uses, especially medical;

Dickson & Dickson[14] Scottish & Romano/Scottish archaeobotany;

School of Scottish Studies[48] oral history often medical;

Grieve[24] and Grigson[26] general historical uses and other matters;

Chevallier[12] Stuart[54] and Bown[7] general medical matters;

Manniche[41] matters relating to early Egyptian, Greek and Roman uses of herbs.

Marsh Woundwort

Woundwort has antiseptic properties and the leafy plant is said to have been used as a wound dressing, probably along with the highly absorbent sphagnum mosses, to staunch wounds on Scottish battlefields over one thousand years ago.

A Garden of Herbs

2.
Culinary Uses of Herbs

Who first used herbs as food or to preserve or to disguise a rancid taste in food before refrigeration is not known. Biblical references tell us that herbs and spices had such high value that they were used as tax payments and that among the gifts the Queen of Sheba took to King Solomon were herb seeds along with Arabian spices. (The spice pepper was so popular and so expensive that it was called black gold, and nutmegs, bought in the Spice Islands and sold in London had a 60,000% mark-up![14] Nutmeg was indeed so rare and valuable that people murdered for it.*)

Opium Poppy

The Romans introduced to Britain many of the herbs we use today such as dill, opium poppy seeds and parsley – perhaps they found our food rather bland. Pliny referred to the Roman custom of sprinkling bread dough with poppy seeds, and opium poppy seeds were found at the Roman fort at Bearsden, near Glasgow. The cookery book that goes under the name of the first century AD Apicius[1] suggests a sophisticated palate.

The early post-Roman peoples of Scotland appear, from skeletal remains, to have been reasonably fit so their diet must have been fairly good. Certainly, according to later records,[45] a diet recommended to patients in the Highlands of 'barley-water, pomegranate wine, soup made with almonds, spinach etc', seems good by any standards. Poorer people may have subsisted on a diet of barley (perhaps as barley broth) and oats (a Roman addition to the diet) with kale and leeks in season and some salted meat. Excavated sites have, however, shown that a range of seabirds, including even the great auk (which survived in Scotland until 1813) and fish such as turbot, halibut and eel, with shellfish like oysters were common. Deer, goat and wild boar were also common and vegetables appear to have been grown.

From the number of herbs, both medicinal and culinary, found at monastic excavations, it seems that early people did use many herbs. We know about these herbs from looking at pollen and fragments of plant remains found in middens at sites of excavations. During Medieval times in Scotland, we know that 'imported' herbs were well-known because they were part of the pharmacopoeia.[5] There has been a well-established oral tradition, as well as written sources, regarding the uses of herbs.[48] Gerard (1597), the respected writer on herbs, noted that many, *eg* parsley, were used to flavour food. It is interesting how many culinary herbs are also medicinal. Perhaps our ancestors learned to use as food herbs that had medicinal value.

Today many herbs are widely available and people are interested to know more about their culinary uses, as they have become an important part of our diet. Ethnic influences and travel have had a profound effect on modern cooking. Diet today is often less good than it could be considering the range of foods available, because processing, preserving and refining methods to make food look and keep better often destroy many valuable ingredients, such as vitamins. People are interested in enhancing the palatability of their food, as can be seen from the number of herbs being bought in supermarkets. Intensive farming methods of the last fifty years are being forced to change to take into account the desire for more nutritious food.

At the same time, however, all things natural are not necessarily good for us, as some would have us believe. Care must be taken in how we use these readily available herbs. It is essential to learn about the herbs you use, as over-use can at times be dangerous and many are poisonous in large quantities. Even common parsley can be dangerous, if taken in excess, when it is potentially damaging to the liver.

Fresh herbs are always to be preferred in salads and even in cooking, but one can freeze small amounts for several weeks without losing too much flavour. Mixtures of herbs are often sold for specific uses; fines herbes composed of chopped parsley, chervil, tarragon and chives are used in soups, sauces, omelettes and cream cheeses. Bouquet garni is made of a few parsley stalks and sprigs of thyme, (a small sprig of marjoram is optional) and a bay leaf. This may be added to stocks, stews or put into birds before roasting.

ACHILLEA MILLEFOLIUM
YARROW

In Sweden, yarrow is called 'field hop', as it has been used in the manufacture of beer. Linnaeus, the famous eighteenth century Swedish botanist, noted that beer thus brewed was more intoxicating than when hops were used.[24] Young leaves, finely chopped with plantain, watercress and cucumber, dressed with lemon, oil and a little apple juice make a delicious salad.

ACORUS CALAMUS
SWEET-FLAG

Because sweet-flag, especially the rhizome, smells and tastes like orange peel it has been candied and has a pleasant perfumed flavour. The Indian candied 'root' is said to have a stronger and more agreeable flavour than the European one.[24]

AEGOPODIUM PODAGRARIA
GROUND-ELDER
BISHOP'S-WEED, GOUTWEED

The Romans introduced ground-elder into Britain.[29] Its popularity later declined but the plant did not! Eating the fresh young leaves cooked as a green vegetable, or using them in salads, is one way of coming to terms with it in the garden. The cooked leaves taste similar to spinach, though they are a bit stringier.

ALLIUM SATIVUM
GARLIC

Garlic's flavour is best developed in a warm sunny country. It has been widely used since the time of the ancient Egyptians. Parsley is supposed to reduce its effect

on the breath, or cloves can be swallowed whole.

ALLIUM CEPA
ONION

Onions have a long history as food for man and have been in use since the time of the Pharaohs.

ALLIUM SCHOENOPRASUM
CHIVES

These are one of the most useful of all kitchen herbs, because they can be cut and still keep growing. Chives are good with new potatoes and in salads.

ALLIUM TUBEROSUM
GARLIC CHIVES

An interesting herb that combines the flavours of garlic and chives.

ALLIUM URSINUM
WILD GARLIC RAMSONS

In Europe the leaves are used in many recipes; in France, where wild garlic is not as common as in Scotland, they are much prized in place of lettuce in sandwiches and are used in salads. An interesting pesto is made in Austria from the leaves: Wild Garlic Pesto 50g sesame seeds (lightly toasted) are blended with 150g good cold-pressed olive oil, then gradually 150g finely chopped garlic leaves are added. Chopped hazelnuts can be used in place of sesame seeds.

Ransoms

ALOYSIA TRIPHYLLA
LEMON VERBENA

Fresh or dried leaves of lemon verbena are used as a tea for indigestion, and finely chopped young leaves can be used sparingly to give a lemon flavour to drinks, cakes and fruit puddings. Try adding to pot-pourris or using them in a herb pillow.

ALTHAEA OFFICINALIS
MARSH-MALLOW

As a vegetable, the Romans considered marsh-mallow to be a great delicacy. The roots were originally used to make the famous sweet. In France, the young tops and tender leaves of marsh mallow are eaten, uncooked, in spring salads. The dried roots are still sold as a 'teether' for babies. They are hard enough for the baby to chew, yet slowly soften as the mucilage is released, which has the added advantage of calming the stomach. The sweet sold today is a mixture of flour, gum, egg albumin but contains no marsh-mallow.[24]

ANETHUM GRAVEOLENS
DILL

As early as the third century AD the Egyptians were using dill. Fragments of seeds were found at a Roman fort near Glasgow.[14] Seeds and leaves are used in pickling cucumbers (called dill pickle). Dill leaves are good in fish sauces and in salads. It is an essential herb in the preparation of gravadlax (sweet-cured salmon). The seed is used whole or ground in soups, fish dishes, cabbage, apple pies, cakes and bread. In Hungarian cooking the feathery leaves of dill are very commonly used; for example, it is excellent with grated marrow and sour cream.

ANGELICA ARCHANGELICA
GARDEN ANGELICA

Angelica is best known for its young stalks and stems which are candied and used as cake decoration, having a pleasant liquorice-like flavour. It was used in flavouring and confectionary in ancient times before sugar was available. The leaves, fresh or dried, make a refreshing tisane, resembling China tea. Angelica is also an important ingredient of liqueurs such as benedictine and some aperitifs, and its seeds are used in the preparation of vermouth, chartreuse and absinthe. The seeds can be used in making stuffing for goose.

ANTHRISCUS CEREFOLIUM
GARDEN CHERVIL

Chervil is one of the traditional ingredients in fines herbes and it is an important culinary herb in France. It is one of the best herbs to grow in boxes as it gives green leaves all winter if transferred to a warm green-house. Use leaves generously in salads, sauces, vegetables, chicken, white fish and egg dishes. They are particularly good spread over glazed carrots, tomatoes and peas. Always add near the end of the cooking to avoid loss of flavour.

APIUM GRAVEOLENS
WILD CELERY

Celery was used in medicine in ancient Egypt as a slimming herb.[41] Seeds of wild celery were found at the Roman fort near Glasgow, so perhaps were used there in cooking.[14] In Medieval times celery was a reputed aphrodisiac and Spanish nuns were forbidden to grow it in their convent gardens.[5] Try adding small amounts of chopped leaves into salads, cream cheese, poultry stuffing, or add to the milk used in cooking fish. The seed can be ground and added to soups, casseroles etc as flavouring and should be added during the last three minutes of cooking time, otherwise the flavour is too strong. Care must be taken not to confuse this plant with other similar-looking very poisonous members of this family, such as hemlock water-dropwort, which is quite common.

ARMORACIA RUSTICANA
HORSE-RADISH
The French name for horse-radish is 'monk's mustard', and Gerard, the sixteenth century herbalist, recommended it in preference to mustard. The grated root is used in horse-radish sauce: it is very pungent but good combined with grated apple and cream. The young leaves can be used in salads.

ARTEMISIA ABSINTHIUM
WORMWOOD ABSINTHE
This herb contains several substances which adversely affect the body, including a hallucinogen, and it is used to produce some of the strongest and most dangerous alcoholic drinks. For this reason absinthe was banned in some countries, especially as it can become addictive.

ARTEMISIA DRACUNCULUS
TARRAGON
This herb has been known here since the sixteenth century. The leaves are rich in iodine, mineral salts and vitimin C. Use sparingly in béarnaise, tartar and hollandaise sauces to serve with mild-flavoured vegetables like marrow and artichoke. Add shredded leaves to avocado fillings, salad dressings and to omelettes; leaves can also be used in herb butter for vegetables, steaks and grilled fish. Try rubbing on roast chicken or mixing with stuffing. Tarragon vinegar is prepared by steeping the fresh herbs in white wine vinegar. French cooks usually mix their mustard with tarragon vinegar.

ASPARAGUS OFFICINALIS
ASPARAGUS
As a vegetable it was much esteemed by the Greeks and Romans as early as 200BC.[1] A prostrate form of asparagus grows in Cornwall, and, although garden asparagus is not native, it grew in Tudor gardens.[26] Gerard mentions that forced asparagus was supplied to the London market in 1670.[24] The tender asparagus used today grows well if stems are protected from light.

BETULA
BIRCH
Birch sap wine, sparkling or still, is excellent: up to two litres of sap can be tapped in a warm day. It has long been popular with home wine makers, and is made by Moniack Castle Wineries near Inverness. Birch is

the favoured wood in Scotland for smoking haddock.[5]

Borago officinalis
BORAGE

Almost all the historical allusions to this plant refer to it as giving happiness and driving away melancholy. Certainly it is used in a variety of alcoholic drinks and is still an ingredient of many summer 'cups'. The flowers are used to decorate wine cups. It is loved by bees, and makes excellent honey. Borage is a traditional addition to Pimm's. The leaves are succulent and tender when young. They can be chopped in salads, salad dressings, and added to pea and bean soups. As there are known toxins in borage it is advisable not to take too much even of the herbal tea.

Calendula officinalis
POT MARIGOLD

The flower petals give a delicate flavour and good colour to salads and omelettes; can be used instead of saffron, which is expensive, in rice; and was formerly used as colouring for cheese and butter.

Calluna vulgaris
HEATHER

The flowers can be used to make a herb tea. Heather honey is much prized and heather ale is an ancient drink. According to a sixteenth-century writer, Dr John Bellenden, *'The Pichtis maid of this herbe, sum time, ane richt delicius and hailsum drink. . . Noctheless, the maner of the making of it perist, be exterminatioun of the said Pichtis out of Scotland'.*[14]

Heather ale, as deduced from pollen at the Neolithic settlements on the Hebridean island of Rum, needs further evaluation.[14] It was once one of the staple drinks of the Highlands. It is possible that the first *uisgebeatha* (Gaelic for whisky) was produced by condensation from this. When Thomas Pennant (*A Tour of Scotland in 1769*) visited Islay he found the islanders made ale from 'the tops of young heather, mixed with a third part of malt and a few hops'. An experimental batch of heather ale was made recently by the distillers, William Grant and Sons – the results were said to be non-toxic and quite palatable.

Carum carvi
CARAWAY

Caraway was not recorded until 1375, but was grown as a crop in England by the sixteenth century. Oil, extracted from the seed, is used to make the German liqueur kummel and the spirit schnapps, while the seeds can be sprinkled over rich meats, pork or goose to aid digestion. Raw or infused, seeds can be chewed to aid digestion, promote appetite and to sweeten the breath. They are especially popular in Jewish and East European cuisine in flavouring cakes, bread and cooked apples. A favourite Hungarian meal is cabbage boiled with potatoes and flavoured with caraway, and caraway soup is given to invalids. Sugar-coated seeds are also popular as digestive comfits. The seeds are used in Britain to flavour soups, bread, cakes, biscuits and apple pies, and the young leaf can be used in salads. The roots are fragrant and in earlier times were used as a substitute for parsnip, to which they have a superior flavour.[14]

CHAMAEMELUM NOBILE
CHAMOMILE

A common plant of early physic gardens as early as 1289 and has been in use since the time of the early Egyptians. Chamomile tea is popular today as an aid to digestion, especially after heavy meals. In the children's story of Peter Rabbit by Beatrice Potter, Peter was given chamomile tea by his mother when he had stolen and eaten too many of the gardener's vegetables and had a sore stomach! This was my introduction to chamomile tea!

CHENOPODIUM BONUS-HENRICUS
GOOD-KING-HENRY FAT HEN

This was an important crop in the Bronze Age, being a rather bland-tasting, but pleasantly textured, green vegetable. Today it grows mainly in waste ground in villages where it was cultivated up to a century ago as a pot-herb. In Germany it is said to have been used to fatten poultry and was called *Fette Henne*, hence one of its names. In Lincolnshire it is still eaten in place of spinach. If the young shoots are peeled and boiled when about five inches high they taste like asparagus. Today it is undergoing a revival in herb gardens.

CORIANDRUM SATIVUM
CORIANDER

The Latin word *sativum* means cultivated which suggests coriander may have been grown since early times. It is mentioned in Sanskrit texts, on Egyptian papyri and in the Bible, where it is compared with Manna. The Romans combined it with cumin and vinegar, to preserve meat and brought it to northern Europe. The cookery book by the Roman Apicius[1] gives recipes for: 'fish with coriander', 'parsnips in a coriander and chive sauce' and 'lentils and chestnuts in a coriander wine sauce'. Seeds were found at the Roman fort near Glasgow. The Chinese believed it conferred immortality, and in the Middle Ages it was put in love potions as an aphrodisiac. The root is cooked and eaten as a vegetable: fresh leaves are widely used as flavouring in stews, sauces and salads. Seeds are used as a spice or condiment, for example in tomato chutney, ratatouille and curries; also in apple pies. Coriander root, crushed with garlic, gives the distinctive flavour of Thai food.

CRATAEGUS MONOGYNA
HAWTHORN

In Scotland a small number of jam-making companies use hawthorn berries in jams and preserves, for instance in mixes known as hedgerow fruits. The flowers and fruits may also be used in the preparation of fruit wines in the UK. Hawthorn flower wine is light and pleasant and has a delicate vanilla bouquet.

Coriander

CRITHMUM MARITIMUM
ROCK SAMPHIRE

This was grown as a kitchen herb in 1598.[24] Its seedpods are used for sauces, pickles and salads. Samphire can be preserved in strong brine; just before use it should be rinsed then put into the best vinegar.

Saffron Crocus

CROCUS SATIVUS
SAFFRON CROCUS

Saffron was from very early times imported for culinary and medicinal purposes. It is very expensive because the part of the flower used is the stigma (the female part) and very approximately, 60,000 stigmas are in a pound of saffron.[24] Such was its standing as a drug that there were very severe penalties imposed on anyone adulterating it. Hans Kolbele, in Germany, was buried alive in 1456 with his impure drug.[49] One must buy saffron from a reputable source. It is used in many dishes, both for taste and for its yellow colour (often replaced by the less expensive tumeric). It makes a delicious tea with cardamon and cinnamon and is also used in some liqueurs. (*see* Aromatic section)

CYNARA CARDUNCULUS
GLOBE ARTICHOKE

One of the world's oldest vegetables, this was introduced both as a vegetable and an ornamental (the flowers look like large thistles) to monastery gardens. The cooked unopened large flower heads and surrounding leaves are a great delicacy.

DIANTHUS CARYOPHYLLUS
CLOVE PINK

This is a wild plant in Southern Europe with clove-scented flowers and is the ancestor of the modern garden carnation. Clove pink is used in flavouring beverages, liqueurs and vinegars.

ERUCA VESICARIA sub-species SATIVA
ROCKET

Rocket's peppery tasting leaves have long been eaten on the continent, but have recently become popular here, especially for use in salads and pizzas. For best flavour rocket should be collected before it flowers. It is said to be easy to grow as a salad vegetable.

ERYNGIUM MARITIMUM
SEA-HOLLY

In the 17th century the roots were candied then eaten as a sweetmeat. According to Linnaeus, the young flowering-shoots, when boiled are just like asparagus and as nourishing; and the roots, boiled or roasted, are like chestnuts and are also nutritious. Sea-holly will grow in a herb garden but the roots will not grow as large and fleshy as on the seashore.[24]

FILIPENDULA ULMARIA
MEADOWSWEET

Meadowsweet is currently used in the preparation of fruit wines in Scotland by, for example, Highland Wineries. The flower is used to flavour beers, wines and mead. Gerard (1633) says that *'the floures boiled in wine and drumke do maketh the heart merrie'*.[20] According to Dickson & Dickson[14] the old name for meadowsweet in southern Scotland means 'mead plant'. Extensive research into the types and proportions of pollen found a sticky substance in a funerary beaker from a Bronze Age cist in Fife (dated 1250) that contained immature pollen from unpollinated flowers and mature pollen which could have been picked up by bees in making honey. Other pollen grains found were common ingredients of honey. This led them to conclude that the mixture must have contained a honey drink, perhaps fermented, flavoured with meadowsweet flowers. Experiments by a distillery firm showed that adding meadowsweet flowers to barley ale produced ale that remained drinkable for months. I, myself, tried to make meadowsweet flower wine: it was very potent, though the flavour left something to be desired! More experienced wine makers might make a better wine. The flowers give a slight almond flavour to jams and stewed fruit. The leaf may be added to soup.

FOENICULUM VULGARE
FENNEL

Fennel needs a long warm growing season to attain the best flavour. Chopped leaves are excellent with oily fish, *eg* mackerel and salmon, as they improve their digestibility. The leaves or seeds give an excellent flavour when added to poached fish or in fish sauces, and the leaves make an excellent garnish. Fennel leaves are good in salads and stews, cooked vegetables, and with boiled and buttered new potatoes. Seeds can be used whole or ground to flavour bread, soups or sweet pickles and oil from the seeds is used in liqueur manufacture. Only the seeds are used in Indian cuisine and they are one of the ingredients of *Garum Masala*. They are similar to cumin seeds and are added to spice mixtures and used especially with fish.

FRAGARIA VESCA
WILD STRAWBERRY

Numerous varieties have been developed since cultivation began in the early sixteenth century, but for centuries the wild strawberry was the one which was gathered. The fruit is delicious and the leaves can be used in strawberry leaf tea. However wild strawberries may produce an allergic response in susceptible people.

GALEGA OFFICINALIS
GOAT'S-RUE

It used to be said that goat's-rue promoted the flow of milk in some animals (and in women) and this is reflected in the name gala which is the Greek word for milk.[54] It has been cultivated as cattle feed. The fresh juice extracted from the plant clots milk and may be used in cheese making.

GALIUM ODORATUM
WOODRUFF

When picked and dried woodruff leaves quickly develop the scent of new-mown hay which is soon taken up by liquids. In Germany a special

Wild Strawberry

punch used to be made for May Day by steeping woodruff in local wine and flavouring with sliced orange and sugar.[39]

___

GLYCYRRHIZA GLABRA
LIQUORICE

The liquorice that we eat is derived from the sweet root of the plant which contains *glycorrhizin*, said to be fifty times sweeter than sugar. Some tobaccos contain ten per cent liquorice, and it is also used to flavour Guinness and other beers. The well-known Pontefract cakes are so called because liquorice was, and still is, grown as a field crop around Pontefract (Yorkshire). As liquorice is a mild laxative do not eat too much. Also if you have high blood pressure, it should be taken in moderation.

___

HELIANTHUS ANNUUS
SUNFLOWER

Sunflower is an important crop in Eastern Europe. Oil in the seed is unsaturated and is widely used as a salad and margarine oil. Sunflower oil is popular for cooking. The seeds are used in animal feed and sold as bird seed, but when roasted they make a tasty snack.

___

HIPPOPHAE RHAMNOIDES
SEA-BUCKTHORN

The berries are used commercially in Eastern Europe, mainly for food. The Scottish Crop Research Institute is promoting the advantages of this plant (which thrives on poor windswept soils) as a commercial crop with high value for food,

soft drinks, cosmetics and for use in the pharmaceutical industry,[5] for example in multivitamin products. The berries have high vitamin content and produce a juice of attractive aroma.

___

HORDEUM VULGARE
BARLEY

Barley is native to the Middle East. It was an important cereal crop dating from the Neolithic period. Originally it was fed to horses and used for medicinal purposes. From early times barley water was taken to soothe the stomach. Large quantities were recommended to be drunk for kidney disease. My mother made a barley water drink during the war as a source of vitamins. Ale made from barley (or bere) was the chief beverage in Medieval times. Monks even had an allowance sufficient to make two gallons each per day because the water supply was not clean. Brewing began very early in Scotland: there are even signs that it may have been carried out at Skara Brae (occupied before the building of the pyramids).[14]

___

HUMULUS LUPULUS
HOP

It was not until the Middle Ages that hops were used in brewing. It was found that the brew originally called 'ale', kept longer when hops were added, and this was called 'beer'. By the end of the sixteenth century beer was the most popular drink in England.[39] Today, in making 'home-brew', the best hop variety is 'fuggle'. The young

A Garden of Herbs

side shoots have long been used in the same way as asparagus.

HYSSOPUS OFFICINALIS
HYSSOP
Hyssop has gone out of favour as a herb because of its strong aromatic flavour. Its smell comes from an oil which can be extracted from the leaves and is valued by manufacturers of liqueurs such as Chartreuse. The flowers make an attractive addition to salads. A few leaves add to the flavour and aid in the digestion of fatty fish and meat.

JUNIPERUS COMMUNIS
JUNIPER
The dried fruits are used to flavour meats (especially game), gin and liqueurs. Only one kilogram of berries is needed to flavour four hundred litres of gin. Juniper was once used as a substitute for pepper, because pepper was very expensive. Roasted berries can be used as a coffee substitute.

LATHYRUS LINIFOLIUS
BITTER-VETCH
The fleshy root-tubers were once gathered for food and were used as a superior substitute for chewing gum with a taste, which lasted well, of wild liquorice.[39] It makes a delicious drink. Sir Robert Sibbald (1641-1722) – the then outstanding authority on medico-botanical matters and co-founder of the Royal College of Physicians of Edinburgh – considered this to be a very important herb. He stated in his *Provision for the Poor in Time of Dearth & Scarcity* (1699) that 'ingestion can eliminate hunger (for an unspecified, yet protracted, length of time) as well as enhancing well-being and endurance'.* If the claims put forward for bitter-vetch as 'very useful in times of food scarcity' are true, it is worthy of growing in herb gardens and of further study today.

LAVANDULA ANGUSTIFOLIA
ENGLISH LAVENDER
Lavender flowers are becoming a very popular addition to food. Marmalade and cakes with lavender flowers added are truly delicious, and are sold by a few small cottage industries in Scotland. Here the more robust Garden Lavender is commonly grown. (*see* Aromatic section)

LAURUS NOBILIS
BAY
This was the laurel tree used to make the victor's 'crown of laurels' in classical times. The tree was once called *baccae lauri* meaning 'noble berry tree', from which the French educational term *baccalaureate* is derived. The fresh dried leaf should be used sparingly in soups, stews, fish dishes or pickles. Bay should not be confused with the garden laurel which is poisonous.

LEVISTICUM OFFICINALE
LOVAGE LOVE PARSLEY
This herb is rarely found wild. Lovage, which is often confused in herbals with Scots lovage, is occasionally seen about the ruins of monasteries and other places where it was grown in olden times as a pot-herb and salad vegetable. The leaves and seeds are used as flavouring, especially

Bitter-vetch

in soup. It has a strong celery-like flavour. The herb had a traditional reputation as a love charm.

LIGUSTICUM SCOTICUM
SCOTS LOVAGE

Scots Lovage or *Shunnis* in Gaelic is a plant highly valued by Highlanders, who eat it raw, or boiled with fish in milk. It is found in rocky places round the coast, especially in Scotland. Young shoots and leaf stalks, eaten raw, have a rather agreeable flavour, not unlike that of celery, but more pungent (now supplanted by celery); they were also used to flavour soups and stews and, some years ago, were still so employed by the country people in parts where the plant was very common. Young stems can be candied like angelica.[24] Seeds can be added to cordials, crushed in bread or pastry, or sprinkled on salads, rice or mashed potatoes. Care must be taken in collecting, as this plant can easily be confused with some very poisonous plants. (*see Apium graveolans*)

MALUS SYLVESTRIS
CRAB APPLE

This is the most important ancestor of the cultivated apple. The fruit makes the well-known crab apple jelly, the shade of which depends on the colour of the fruit. As it is high in pectin it is often added, as a setting agent, when making other jams. It can be roasted and served with meat.

MELISSA OFFICINALIS
BALM

The popularity of this herb is due to the delightful tea made from its dried leaves. It is of wide culinary potential where a delicate lemon flavour is required. It is used in making excellent wines and is an important constituent of several liqueurs. Lemon balm is an important bee plant.

MENTHA
MINTS

Several are native in Scotland and are familiar to us today in the garden and as herbal teas which were popular before the introduction of leaf tea.

MENTHA X PIPERATA
PEPPERMINT

The 'x' in the name shows that this plant is a hybrid. Often hybrids are more robust than the original plants. Oil from peppermint is used as flavouring in sweets, chewing gum and cakes and in dental preparations. Peppermint water ice is delicious. The leaves can be added to fruit juices and fruit salads.

MENTHA PULEGIUM
PENNYROYAL

This strongly flavoured mint is used in stews etc. and to flavour black puddings in Britain and sausages in Spain; however it may not be safe for pregnant women to take too much, as pennyroyal may act to abort a foetus at an early stage in pregnancy. It is a powerful purgative*.

MENTHA X SMITHIANA
RED RARIPILA MINT

The leaves of this hybrid are an important ingredient of mint

Pennyroyal

A Garden of Herbs

sauce and of jelly to accompany lamb, and are used for herb teas and in ice drinks. This mint is also of value commercially in dental preparations and in chewing gum.

MENTHA X SMITHIANA 'MOROCCAN'
MOROCCAN MINT
This is a favourite hardy cultivar.[7] It makes a refreshing herb tea served with honey and is popular with Arab peoples.

MENTHA SPICATA
SPEAR MINT
This common garden mint is used for sauces and jellies and as a salad mixed with yoghurt and cucumber. It goes well with lamb. Spearmint chewing gum is very popular.

MENTHA X VILLOSA
APPLE-MINT
The leaves are delicious in fruit salads, fruit cups and water ices.

MENTHA X VILLOSA
V. ALOPECUROIDES
BOWLES' MINT
This tall vigorous mint has a fine flavour and is one of the best all round mints. The flavour is similar to spearmint but it is more resistant to disease. It is good with potatoes, peas, in lettuce soup or infused with green tea to make a refreshing drink.

Mint Sauce Pick leaves from stalks, mince finely and half-fill a small jam jar. Add one teaspoonful of brown sugar, fill with good vinegar, cover and stand for a while before use.

MEUM ATHAMANTICUM
SPIGNEL BALDMONEY
This plant is native in grassland in the north. Once it was used extensively as a sweet root

vegetable. The feathery foliage adds an aromatic flavour to soups and vegetable dishes; the leaves have a strong smell of parsley.

MONARDA DIDYMA
BERGAMOT BEE BALM
The leaves can be infused as tea and give an Earl Grey flavour to China tea and iced drinks. Flowers are added to salads.

MYRRHIS ODORATA
SWEET CICELY
All parts of the plant taste and smell of aniseed. It is a 'sugar saver' herb and if finely chopped leaves are added they cut down acidity when cooking tart fruits *eg* gooseberries, rhubarb or red currants. The leaves or seeds (while still green) can be used in salads or added to fresh fruit salads and summer drinks, or to the water used to cook cabbage.

OCIMUM BASILICUM
BASIL
Basil is a vital ingredient in Italian cooking, the leaves being used to flavour soups, egg dishes, salads, dressings and poultry, especially as a stuffing for duck. It can also be used with garlic in sauces and it goes particularly well with tomatoes. It makes delicious pesto – pound it with garlic and salt, mix with Parmesan cheese; pine kernels may be added. Fresh basil, now readily available, is much better than the dried herb; other varieties of basil, such as the small pungent Greek basil, are becoming popular pot herbs.

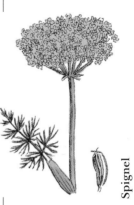

Spignel

OENOTHERA BIENNIS
EVENING-PRIMROSE

Young roots, if boiled, taste like parsnip: pickle and toss in salads. French people use the bright yellow flowers to garnish salads.

ORIGANUM
MARJORAM; OREGANO

The Greeks have given us the name *ore gamos* which means 'joy of the mountain'. Those who know Greece remember its wonderful scent on the hill-sides.

ORIGANUM MARJORANA
SWEET MARJORAM

This is not an annual but is usually treated as such as it does not survive our winters. It is used extensively in Mediterranean countries as a seasoning in cookery as well as in medicine, but it is the cultivated species, *Oregano onites* **Pot Marjoram**, that is mainly used here. Chop it finely for salads and butter sauces for fish. It is widely used for meat dishes and should be added in the last ten minutes of cooking time. It is said to aid digestion. Large quantities are grown and gathered as a cottage industry in the south of England where it is hung up to dry to make marjoram tea.[24]

Marjoram

ORIGANUM VULGARE
WILD MARJORAM; OREGANO

This characteristic herb of Mediterranian cookery does not develop such an earthy fragrance in our cooler climate although it is still an excellent kitchen herb. Use the leaves in salads and sauces and mixed with other herbs to flavour stews etc. Greek people once used it to crown young couples; it was also said to augur happiness to 'the departed' if it grew on their graves.[24]

PAPAVER RHOEAS
COMMON POPPY

There has been a recent resurgence in poppy numbers in Scotland, with the 'set-aside' land policy of the late 1980s.[34] Try sprinkling the seed on bread, cakes or biscuits or use in salads. It is of interest that it was seeds of Opium poppy that were found at the Roman fort near Glasgow. At that time they were probably only used to sprinkle on bread, as was a Roman custom. This custom is again quite popular in Britain today. The seeds of common or opium poppy contain little or no opium when grown in our climate.

PELARGONIUM
GERANIUM

Various scented species of pelargonium or geranium are used for flavouring in sponge cakes, jellies, sorbets and salads. The leaves and flowers can be used in pot pourris.

PERSICARIA BISTORTA
BISTORT

The leaves are still boiled and eaten as greens in parts of England. The flowers and leaves are used in Easter Ledger Pudding, which is eaten in the Lake District as a cleansing bitter dish for Lent.[26] When work on the Flora of Glasgow was being undertaken it was found that bistort was common in Victorian cemeteries, not in older or more modern ones. Perhaps in some way it had another religious significance at that time which is now lost.

Easter Ledger Pudding

Pick young leaves of bistort and drop them with leaves of dandelion, Lady's mantle, or nettle into boiling water and cook for 20minutes. Strain and chop, add a little boiled barley, a chopped hard-boiled egg and seasoning. Heat and press into a pudding basin. Serve with veal and bacon.

PETROSELINUM CRISPUM
PARSLEY

The Greeks planted parsley and rue along the edges of herb beds. They used it medicinally. It appears that the Romans were the first to use it as a food and possibly to introduce it into Britain. They consumed it in quantity, apparently to discourage intoxication at parties and to supress smells. Pliny recommended it to be used in every sauce. Deep-fried it makes an unusual garnish. The variety 'French' is the popular flat parsley.

POTENTILLA ANSERINA
SILVERWEED

According to Beith[5] the tuberous roots were sometimes eaten raw, having a nutty flavour. She considers that it is likely that, before cereals were regularly cultivated in the Highlands, meal made from the dried roots may have been used as part of the staple diet: it was used in times of famine and at the time of the Highland Clearances, as it

was one of the few edible plants disliked by sheep.

PRIMULA VULGARIS
PRIMROSE

The flowers are used candied and in salads. The dried flowers make primrose tea.

PRIMULA VERIS
COWSLIP

The deliciously scented flowers of this once common plant make the most delicate of all country wines. Unfortunately it is difficult to buy true wild cowslip seeds.

PRUNUS PADUS
BIRD CHERRY

Bird cherry fruits are acidic and are added to flavour whisky, gin and other spirits such as Kirsch. There is a reference in *Flora Scotica* (1777) to bird cherry being used in home-made preserves. Moniack Castle produces wild cherry jelly. The Latin *padus* means very hard and according to Pliny cherry wood was used to make paddles for boats.

RHEUM X HYBRIDUM
RHUBARB

The stalks of rhubarb produce the well-liked conserve, and are made into jam, chutney and wine. They can be used to make a delicious fool; add a beaten egg white to sieved, cooked rhubarb and chill before eating. Rhubarb crumble is also very popular. One should not cook rhubarb in an aluminium pot, as, being very acid, it reacts with the metal. The leaves are very poisonous and must not be eaten.

Cowslip

Blackcurrant

RIBES NIGRUM
BLACKCURRANT

John Gerard in his *Generall Historie of Plantes* (1597) described them as 'of a stinking and somewhat loathsome savour'. The fruits he also thought would 'breed worms in the stomach'. Blackcurrant leaves were once important as a substitute for Indian and China tea. During the eighteenth and nineteenth centuries shortages and high prices of tea led to a widespread practice of using them to make substitute blends. Blackcurrant fruits are widely used in jams, drinks, cordials and liqueurs; the leaves also, boiled with sugar, can be used as a flavouring for ice-lollies and cordials.

ROSMARINUS OFFICINALIS
ROSEMARY

This plant was known in Britain by 1375, but not before.[29] Fresh rosemary is used in salads and, sparingly, in a wide range of meat dishes, especially pork and lamb. The leaves are said to aid in the digestion of fats.

RUBUS FRUTICOSUS
BRAMBLE

The fruits of several members of the genus *rubus* are used in the production of wine. Of these, bramble is, perhaps, best known. It is thought that the ancient Greeks were the first to ferment brambles to make wine, but the practice is almost universally European. They are also commonly used in jams etc. and are a good source of vitamin C.

RUBUS IDAEUS
RASPBERRY

A native, which has entered cultivation, has a yellow-berried form that grows in Speyside. Currently it is used by a few companies in the commercial production of wines. The inhabitants of Skye use raspberries for making syrup and alcoholic beverages, the syrup being used as flavouring for whisky and other spirits. A tea made from the leaves was once given to expectant mothers in the Highlands, as it was thought to strengthen the muscles of the womb. The juice of the fruits, slightly distilled, was also used as a refreshing drink (this was considered to be particularly good for patients with a fever).[5]

RUMEX ACETOSA
SORREL; SOOROCKS

In France sorrel is cultivated and is well thought of as a food to eat fresh or cooked, but sorrel is poisonous in large amounts, and the juice will curdle milk. It does make excellent soup, cooked in butter, gently simmered with béchamel sauce, then seasoned.[17]

RUSCUS ACULEATUS
BUTCHER'S-BROOM

It is hard to believe that this plant is a member of the lily family. It looks like a dwarf holly with spiny 'leaves' – really flattened stems – that carry scarlet berries in the middle of the flat 'leaves'. The name came from the fact that sprigs of the spiny stalks were used to clean butchers' blocks and as 'fences'

A Garden of Herbs

to ward off mice! Fresh sprigs were used as meat tenderizers.

SALICORNIA EUROPAEA
GLASSWORT; MARSH SAMPHIRE
This shiny succulent grows on salt-marshes (not in herb gardens) and one should pick only plants that are washed by every tide. They look like plump shiny pipe-cleaners. When gathering, they should be cut with scissors, not pulled out, as it is against the law to up-root wild plants. It contains a large proportion of mineral salts. The fresh plant is diuretic. Wash it well and dry it carefully if you are not cooking it right away. It is becoming popular, eaten raw as a crisp salad plant, or lightly cooked and dipped in melted butter. This plant is moving up-market! It had an honored place in the wedding breakfast of Prince Charles and Princes Diana in 1981, delivered fresh from the Sandringham Estate in Norfolk, and it appears increasingly on the menus of smart restaurants.[39]

SALVIA OFFICINALIS
SAGE
The leaves can be used in sage and onion stuffing and added to roast pork or duck, to counteract the fatty richness. Sage is one of the best herbs to add to tomato and pasta dishes and to sauces when grilling fish. Use it sparingly, as the flavour increases when cooked. Fresh leaves are good in green salads and dressings.

SAMBUCUS NIGRA
ELDER
The flowers, buds and fruits have a wide culinary application eg in wine, pies, jams and chutneys. The flower, added to gooseberry jam and to stewed gooseberries gives them a muscatel flavour and improves their quality; they can also be used in fruit cups. A cordial is made commercially, using wild blossoms infused with sugar-water. Elder flowers make one of the best country wines. The sparkling wine was called elder-flower champagne, but this name is no longer allowed, since the word champagne is reserved for the Champagne district of France. Wine from the fruit is entirely different in appearance and flavour. A sweet honey-flavoured tea is made from the flower heads. Fritters made from elder flowers are excellent.

Elderflower fritters
Pick the flowers when just in bloom, put in a basin with lemon peel, castor sugar, brandy and a few drops of orange flower water and marinade; then add to a thick batter and fry in hot oil for a short time and drain well. Sprinkle with castor sugar.[17]

SATUREJA MONTANA & HORTENSIS
WINTER & SUMMER SAVORY
Savory, with its peppery spiciness, is one of the oldest flavouring herbs. Its oil is used commercially as flavouring. The leaves are an important constituent of salami and are also good in bean dishes to help relieve flatulence.

Glasswort

Sorbus aucuparia
ROWAN

The berries are used for making jelly which goes exceptionally well with game and lamb. Try adding a few crab-apples when making the jelly, to help it to set.

Symphytum officinale
COMFREY

Fresh leaves were used as a vegetable and dried plants as a substitute for tea, however only tea made from the leaves (which contain relatively low levels of alkaloids) is safe.[3]

Tanacetum balsamata
COSTMARY

The fresh or dried leaves can be used in a spring salad and as a flavouring in home made beer, soups, cakes and in pastry.

Tanacetum vulgare
TANSY

Sometimes known as yellow buttons, tansy was used as a moth repellent, and was placed around the home to discourage flies and other insects. From the fifteenth to the nineteenth century 'tansye' was a generic name for any pancake-like food flavoured with bitter herbs; tansy's bitter leaves were used in a Lenten dish to kill off 'phlegm and worms'. Young leaves, before they become bitter, can be chopped in salads or cooked like spinach; young stems can be blanched as you would asparagus. In the days before refrigerators it was rubbed over meat to preserve it.

Taraxacum officinale
DANDELION

In France an 'improved', less bitter variety of the plant is cultivated. There the leaves are blanched and used in salads or in cooking; try frying in deep fat – they taste delicious. Dandelion wine is also excellent. When coffee was scarce or expensive the best coffee substitute was considered to be the powdered roasted roots of dandelion, which were also thought to settle upset stomachs. During World War II, at the RAF base near Tain, Ross-shire, an unusual use was made of dandelion stalks. The servicemen had access to old bike parts from which they could 'cobble together' useable bikes, but the shortage of valve tubes for the tyres was rather a problem and forced the men to improvise, using the dandelion stalks!*

Thymus vulgaris
THYME

The flavour of thyme varies in strength according to soil and climate – thymes coming from the Mediterranean having a more powerful flavour. For dishes where the characteristic flavour is especially important it is worth buying good quality imported dried herbs. This thyme is the most useful from a culinary point of view and, given a well-drained soil and a sunny position, it is one of the best winter herbs, having a strong aromatic flavour; ideal in soups and stews and able to keep its flavour in long slow cooking, as in pot roasts.

Thyme

A Garden of Herbs

THYMUS X CITRIODORUS
LEMON THYME

Mix with parsley in place of lemon peel for stuffing chicken.

TROPAEOLUM MAJUS
NASTURTIUM

The fresh leaves and flowers can be used in salads. The seeds can be preserved in vinegar as a caper substitute. A little added sugar is said to improve the flavour.

TROPAEOLUM TUBEROSUM
TUBEROUS NASTURTIUM

The tuber multiplies in the same way as a potato does and it has a peppery flavour when fresh, but vanilla-like when cooked. The tuberous nasturtium grows well in Scotland.

URTICA DIOICA
NETTLE

Nettles were a very early source of food. The Romans used them, and during the Irish Famine and the two world wars they were widely cooked and eaten. They were an important item of diet, especially in the spring, in the Highlands, supplying vitamin C and roughage. They are today often found growing beside old dwellings in places where nitrogenous rubbish had been left, and no doubt were always around where swill was deposited. Traditionally they were eaten in a kind of soup with oatmeal. A recipe for a soup called St Columba's broth is take 'a handful of very young nettles per person, boil, drain, chop and return to pot with water and milk. Reheat, sprinkle with fine oatmeal, stir till thickens'.[39] Nettles three/four inches high should be used. The shoots and leaves can be used to make beer.

VACCINIUM MYRTILLUS
BILBERRY; BLAEBERRY

When picked fresh, blaeberries are very much appreciated for their flavour and are a good source of vitamins. They are excellent cooked in pies, to which apples can be added if you tire of collecting the blaeberries! Today in shops we mostly find the larger American bilberry.

VACCINIUM VITIS-IDEA
COWBERRY

A rather tart fruit in conserves and syrups, the red berries of cowberry add to the flavour of certain liqueurs. Liqueurs made from cowberry and other mountain berries such as cloudberry and blaeberry are very popular in Scandinavia.

VALERIANA OFFICINALIS
VALERIAN

The leaves have been used in salads or cooked as a vegetable and the root used in soup. Valerian is one of the Findhorn Flower Essences, made by the Bach 'sun-infusion' method. Flower remedies are taken to 'encourage positive qualities and to address emotional, psychological and soul issues'. Valerian as a vegetable or as a medicine should be used with caution (*see* Medical herbs). Extracts are used commercially in flavouring ice-cream, soft drinks, beer and are especially important in apple flavours.[7]

Sweet Violet

VIOLA ODORATA
SWEET VIOLET

The cultivated flower is widely used in a candied form by the confectionary industry *eg* to decorate chocolates.

Notes

Page 57 * Milton, G. (1999) *Nathaniel's Nutmeg* Hodder and Stoughton, London

Page 67 * Folio Issue 1 (2000) *A Marvellous Plant* (National Library of Scotland)

Page 68 * Gibson, J. pers. com. (*see Mentha puligium* pennyroyal in Medical section)

Page 74 * P. Andrews, Southampton (1996)

Principle books or articles consulted

Grieve[24] very comprehensive encyclopedia of all aspects of herbs;

Dickson & Dickson[14] Scottish & Romano/Scottish archaeobotany;

Beith[5] Scottish/Highland uses of herbs;

Mabey[39] covers folk history of native and naturalised plants and their uses;

Grigson[2] general history of herbs and their uses;

School of Scottish Studies[48] oral history;

Manniche[41] matters relating to early Egyptian, Greek and Roman uses of herbs;

Bown[7] a Royal Horticultural Society encyclopedia of herbs and their uses;

Stuart[54] useful general information about herbs

3.

Aromatic, Cosmetic and other uses of Herbs

The book of Genesis tells how 'the Lord God planted a garden in the east, in Eden' and a river which watered the Garden, also watered Havilah where was found *bdellium*. This is thought to be the aromatic resin, called in the Scriptures, myrrh.[41]

Perfumed oils were known to the ancient civilisations of Egypt and Persia. As can be seen from hieroglyphs of about 3100BC, the Egyptians were already making cosmetics and perfumes. A fascinating glimpse of people preparing unguents (aromatic substances) is shown in a wall-painting from a Theban tomb dated from about 1400BC. Before distillation was known, around 400BC, scents apparently were extracted by steeping plants and aromatic wood in oils. To illustrate the scale of perfume production, in one recipe for oil of lilies, it says 'take two thousand lilies'. Egyptian ladies appear to have dyed their fingernails and painted their lips and a picture on a papyrus shows a lady applying lip gloss. They used rouge (traces of which have survived on mummies) and the court ladies used green eye shadow, made of malachite. Indeed they valued cosmetics and scents so highly that the wealthy were buried with ornate vases of beauty products. Large quantities of frankincense and myrrh were imported for temple worship, funerary rituals, cosmetics and medicine. Perfumes from the tomb of Tutankhamun were still faintly fragrant after more than 3,000 years. When Cleopatra went to meet Anthony she had the royal purple sails of her barge saturated with perfume. The priests of ancient Egypt used fragrances like cedar oil, in religious ceremonies, in medicine and in embalming. These early

Egyptians had prototypes of most modern skin preparations, and were lavish with their use of perfumes.[41]

The ancient Persians gave us the first gardens of aromatic and scented herbs under shade trees in peaceful surroundings. They brought preservation of flowers to a fine art. One method they used to enjoy roses out of season was to pick the buds and store them in sealed jars in a cool place for use when required.[41]

The Greeks later studied the art of perfumery; wealthy Greeks applying a different perfume to each part of their body. They, in turn, passed their love of cosmetics and scents to the Romans with whom bath oils were especially popular. Julius Caesar, believing this to be effeminate, published a decree forbidding the sale of scented oils, but the use of oils and cosmetics continued, and gradually spread to the far corners of the Roman Empire.

The Koran describes paradise as being filled with nymphs created out of musk. So fond of musk were the followers of Mohammed that they mixed it with the mortar used to build their mosques. The lingering perfume can still be detected.

In China, Confucius (c.600BC) recorded that on New Year's day, houseboats and temples were hung about with fragrant blossoms of peach, magnolia and jasmine and there was an enormous consumption of incense sticks – still very popularly used in the home. Unopened buds, mainly of jasmine, were picked before dawn and sold for decorating the hair of Chinese girls. The petals were used to perfume tea, and this is still done today. Buds were strung into garlands for wearing. When in India recently, I saw, in every town, flower-sellers making up necklaces of jasmine buds to sell; a custom which may have spread from China.

The ancient Britons may not have bathed as much as the Romans, for whom bathing was a social event. The Britons painted their bodies, possibly in interesting patterns, with woad, and did appear to be war-like to the Roman, when they first arrived. Perhaps, however, it was a beauty preparation, as some kind of protection against malignant influences. The use of perfumes seems to have disappeared after the Romans left Britain. Hygiene, however, appears to have been considered important in Scotland – medicated baths often being mentioned in early Gaelic literature. There is also mention of taking baths for leprosy and other skin diseases.[5]

By Medieval times it was believed that many aromatic plants

were effective in keeping away disease like the plague. People carried pomanders made with oranges and cloves and aromatic herbs to ward off smells and to guard against infection. Plants were strewn on the floor to make the house and church more pleasant-smelling and hygienic. Aromatic herbs were used to perfume the body – perhaps to disguise the fact that baths were rarely taken. Beauty products became so popular that in 1770 a bill was introduced by the English Parliament to permit a marriage to be dissolved if the man was deceived into it by 'scents, paints, cosmetic washes.'

Today herbs are the main source of perfumes and fragrances. Modern perfumery is concentrated in Grasse in southern France, where there are plantations of roses, violets, jasmine, mimosa and orange-blossom. Bergamot from the East, lavender and peppermint from England are exported to France. Secret mixtures of herbs are used to create the top perfumes. Synthetic essences were introduced at the end of the nineteenth century, but natural oils still predominate in quality perfumes. There has been a resurgence of interest in herbal oils with the modern popularity of aromatherapy.

To be surrounded by the sweet scent of herbs can be the perfect antidote to overwork and stress, as breathing slows and deepens our tense muscles should relax. Some scented herbs have an ancient reputation for improving memory, and some are currently being investigated. To bring their uses right up to date, some appear to reduce electromagnetic pollution from computers.[9]

Magnolia

Anita Pearman

Aromatic & Cosmetic Uses of Herbs

ACHILLEA MILLEFOLIUM
YARROW
The flowers have a musky smell and the fern-like leaves a refreshing scent like feverfew. Some of the coloured varieties are very attractive and they last well when cut. An infusion is astringent and cleanses and beautifies the skin – especially an oily skin.

ACORUS CALAMUS
SWEET-FLAG
Sweet-flag was first grown in England about 1600AD The scent of sweet-flag, especially of the root, is like orange peel. Because of this, in the seventeenth century, it was strewn on floors in abbeys and cathedrals at festivals and often in wealthy private homes instead of the ordinary rushes to mask smells. It was scarce as it only grew in East Anglia, so was expensive. One of the charges of extravagance laid against Cardinal Wolsey was that he ordered the floors of his palace to be covered too often with these rushes. They were strewn on the floor of Norwich Cathedral until recently at festivals.[24] The plants, mainly the roots, contain a volatile oil that is distilled and used in perfumery and is an ingredient of one of the most popular of modern perfumes, Chypre.

AGASTACHE FOENICULUM
ANISE HYSSOP
Anise-flavoured herb with anise-scented leaves, used by native Americans as a tea. It was widely planted by bee-keepers in North America in the 1870s to produce a fine honey with a slight aniseed flavour.

ALOYSIA TRIPHYLLA
LEMON VERBENA
This South American plant was introduced to Europe by the Spaniards and was once used to give a lemon scent to fingerbowls at banquets. It has a rich smell of lemon and is used in pot-pourris and perfumery, especially in the expensive Eau de Verveine. Its use declined following evidence that it may sensitize the skin to sunlight. The leaves will keep their perfume for years, and should be gathered at flowering time.[24] The plant needs shelter from cold winds in winter.

ANETHUM GRAVEOLENS
DILL
The Latin word *graveolens* means heavily scented. Dill has long been used in perfume mixes. Today the unripe flower-head is an important flavouring in pickled gherkins. (*see* Culinary section)

ANTHRISCUS CEREFOLIUM
GARDEN CHERVIL
The handsome fern-like leaves of this hardy annual have a delicate anise scent and flavour.

APIUM GRAVEOLENS
WILD CELERY
This wild variety of celery has celery scented and flavoured leaves. The seeds are also used in flavourings. The plant is frequently mentioned in Egyptian texts as being used to form a garland for mummies made of leaves with petals of the

blue lotus flower dating from about 1,000 BC. One is on show in a Cairo Museum. Garlands of scented flower buds are commonly made today in parts of India and sold by the roadside, the flower buds being picked before dawn and stored in cool wet blankets until ready to be threaded for sale, just as was done in China and Egypt centuries ago.

AQUILEGIA VULGARIS
COLUMBINE

The name *Aquilegia* is derived from the Latin *aquila* (an eagle) because part of the flower resembles an eagle's talons. The popular name also comes from a Latin *columba* (a dove or pigeon), from the idea that the flowers resemble the flight of these birds. It is a favourite old-fashioned garden flower mentioned in many old flower books. Columbine used to be used medicinally, but, according to Linnaeus, the famous Swedish botanist, some children were poisoned when given too large a dose.

ARTEMISIA ABROTANUM
SOUTHERNWOOD

The name in Anglo Saxon means 'midge-plant', and it has been cultivated since antiquity to repel insects and contagion. Southernwood was planted beside roads for Roman soldiers to place in their sandals on long marches. Its dried leaves placed in wardrobes in muslin bags will deter moths, hence the French name *garde-robe*(the French word for wardrobe). It was at one time incorporated in nosegays against the plague. Southernwood is

today used in some hair lotions. There is a beautiful silver form of southernwood.

CALENDULA OFFICINALIS
POT MARIGOLD

The flowers, as a potion, were used as a hair rinse to brighten fair hair. To add colour to salads, collect the flowers on a dry day, spread on sheets of paper, then dry in a current of warm air in the shade.

CARUM CARVI
CARAWAY

Its oil, especially present in the seeds, is used for flavouring and perfumery. The leaf can be infused as a hair tonic and conditioner.

CEDRONELLA CANARIENSIS
BALM-OF-GILEAD

The leaves of this shrub have a strong scent of camphor, especially when bruised. They are dried for pot-pourris and add a musky, smoky scent. This plant is incorrectly called Balm-of-Gilead. The true perfumed resin is produced by some members of the poplar family – not much used today.

CHAMAEMELUM NOBILE
CHAMOMILE

Has long been used in baths, face oils, as an inhalant, in massage and as a room fragrance. In beauty salons chamomile tea is often served to relax facial muscles. It blends well with geranium and lavender in aromatherapy. It is valued for its sweet apple-scented leaves. The soothing and cleansing properties make a good skin

Columbine

wash. An infusion makes an excellent hair rinse, lightens fair hair and is good for the scalp. In Elizabethan gardens Chamomile lawns were popular, and a favourite feature were chamomile seats. (currently enjoying a revival) The non-flowering variety *Treneague*, discovered early last century, creates a dense scented lawn, requiring no mowing. Sir Francis Drake is reputed to have played his famous game of bowls on a chamomile lawn.[39]

CLINOPODIUM GRANDIFLORUM
GREATER CALAMINT

The lilac-purple flowers have a delicious minty smell and the delicate scented foliage makes a refreshing herb tea.

CONVALLARIA MAJALIS
LILY-OF-THE-VALLEY

The flowering head of this plant is pure white with a sweet spicy perfume. It contains a volatile oil, rich in *farnesol*, used in perfumery and was used in snuff. The flowers of lily of the valley were 'forced' to come early and these were popular as winter decoration in Victorian times.

CROCUS SATIVUS
SAFFRON CROCUS

Saffron was the Karkon of the Song of Solomon in the Old Testament. It was one of the most cherished of all perfumes, by the Romans who had their apartments and banqueting halls strewn with the flowers, and the most prized essence was made from the stigmas (*see* Culinary

section). The stigma only ripens in hot dry regions, although in the fourteenth century, when it is believed the weather was warmer here, it grew in Saffron Walden. The crest of Saffron Walden has this crocus in full colour, showing its 'golden' stigmas'. Perhaps it was sold at Saffron Hill in London. The idea of growing saffron was introduced by the Secretary of State of Edward III in 1330 in order to initiate a new industry for the villagers of Saffron Walden.[49]

DIANTHUS CARYOPHYLLUS
CLOVE PINK

From this plant many of the new varieties of hardy border carnations have been raised. A number of these carry the rich clove perfume of the parent, however almost no perfume is present in the yellow or orange-flowering varieties.[14] The word carnation has the same origin as coronation as they were used to make celebratory garlands.

FILIPENDULA ULMARIA
MEADOWSWEET

No plant was held in greater esteem in Elizabethan times and it was said to be the Queen's favourite strewing herb. It has an aromatic root-stock. Although the fresh flowers have a slightly sickly smell the leaves are pleasantly aromatic especially when trodden upon. This is due to the presence of oil of wintergreen. It can also be used to scent linen and the dried flowers used in pot-pourris.

FOENICULUM VULGARE
FENNEL

The bright green aromatic feathery foliage, golden yellow flowers and the delightful aniseed scent and flavour make this a very popular garden plant. The leaves remain aromatic if dried in a warm airy place in the dark, which is the best way preserve the scent and the colour. Fennel has been used in perfumery and in the manufacture of liqueurs. *Foeniculum purpureum* is a bronze-coloured variety.

FRAGARIA VESCA
WILD STRAWBERRY

Wild strawberry is native to Britain. In addition to the aroma of its ripening fruits its leaves also release a musky smell when dying, and this may be extracted. A decoction of the leaf acts as an astringent for an oily skin.

GALIUM ODORATUM
WOODRUFF

The scent which develops when woodruff is picked and dried lasts well. Dried bunches were hung in wardrobes until quite recently, by country people, to deter moths and to scent clothes. It was a favorite strewing herb in Medieval times, for its scent and as a protection against infections. It has also been used in perfumery.

GALIUM VERUM
LADY'S BEDSTRAW

Like woodruff this dries to a scent of new-mown hay and its frothy yellow flower is honey-scented when fresh, like other bedstraws. The name probably derives from the old custom of including it in straw mattresses.

GEUM URBANUM
WOOD AVENS HERB BENNET

This was called the Blessed Herb (*Herba benedicta*), because in former times its strongly aromatic roots were thought to protect against evil spirits, and drive away witches. The *Ortus Sanitatis* by Johann von Cube, printed in 1491, states: 'Where the root is in the house, Satan can do nothing and flies from it.'[24] The roots dried and tied in bundles impart a delicious aromatic flavour if cooked with apples.

HAMAMELIS VIRGINIANA
VIRGINIAN WITCH HAZEL

This is a source of the witch hazel of commerce, used in beauty parlours everywhere. It is perhaps the most widely used astringent in most toning lotions.

HELIANTHUS ANNUUS
SUNFLOWER

Sunflower comes from Peru where it is the emblem of the Sun God and to be found carved on the walls of Inca temples. It is a decorative rather than a perfume plant.

HESPERIS MATRONALIS
DAME'S-VIOLET

This attractive pale pink flower belongs to the same family as wallflower and stock, and has a similar fragrance. The smell is strongly of violets, with, in the evening, an additional hint of cloves. In 1930 it was rarely found outside gardens but now it has become well established on waste ground, indeed it is extremely common in the far north, especially on the Orkney Isles.

HYSSOPUS OFFICINALIS
HYSSOP

As a kitchen herb hyssop has gone a bit out of favour because the flavour is so strong, but it makes a lovely edging or border plant having varieties with blue, red and white flowers. Bees love it and the smell of the honey is very good. Its strong aromatic smell comes from an oil that can be extracted from the leaves and is valued by perfumiers and manufacturers of liqueurs such as Chartreuse.

IRIS GERMANICA V. FLORINTINA
ORRIS

The Florentine iris is one of the oldest flowers in cultivation. It is said to be the model for the Fleur-de-lys of heraldry. When dried and ground, orris root (really the underground stem) produces a powder possessing the fragrance of violets, used by the Victorians as face powder. It is one of the chief ingredients of the famous perfume Frangipani and used in many other perfumes, cosmetics and in pot-pourris. It is used as a fixative in the manufacture of perfumes.

LAURUS NOBILIS
BAY

In Roman times it was used as the 'Victor's laurel' being called *laurus* from *laudare*, 'to praise'. The aromatic fragrance of bay has long had a reputation for cleansing the air and keeping away pestilence. It is said that the Emperor Claudius moved his court to Laurentium, celebrated for its bay trees, to avoid the plague. Bay is a vital ingredient of *bouquet garni*. Take care not to confuse bay with garden laurel which is poisonous. It is hardy if protected from the worst frosts and winds.

LAVANDULA ANGUSTIFOLIA
ENGLISH LAVENDER

This lavender has an exquisitely scented oil, used in aromatherapy. Lavender, but which one it is not clear, was used to scent and disinfect the hot water of Roman public baths, and was introduced by the Romans to the far corners of the Empire. Muslin bags with dried flowers or lavender oil can be added to baths and are fragrant and refreshing and dried leaves in a herb cushion keep away moths and encourage sleep. The first recipe for lavender oil dates from 1615, and was associated with personal and domestic hygiene. For this reason the name in Elizabethan times for a laundress was *lavandre* (in Latin the word *lavare* means to wash). It is used to mask unpleasant odours in ointments, and as a flavouring agent.[51] Distillation of lavender began early in the seventeenth century in Surrey, still the home of lavender growing, where the world's finest lavender-water is still produced. The flowers of English lavender can be used to make a tonic for sensitive skins as the light oil from them is healing for minor sores.[12]

A Garden of Herbs

LAVANDULA X INTERMEDIA
GARDEN LAVENDER

The quality of the perfume from lavender depends on sunshine so Scottish plants are not the best for perfume, however this more robust hybrid does quite well in Scotland.

LAVANDULA LATIFOLIA
SPIKE LAVENDER

This lavender is unusual in that the scent is pungent and camphoraceous so it is used mainly in cheap perfumes, cleaning products and as an insect repellent.[7] Try a few drops on cotton-wool in a perforated container to keep away flies. Not only are insects affected by the smell, but lions and tigers in a Zoo were said to become quite docile under its influence![24]

LINUM USITATISSIMUM
CULTIVATED FLAX

Linen is woven from the stem fibres, probably the first woven cloth. Egyptian mummies were wrapped in linen. During the second world war it was grown near Glasgow, but although people have looked in places where it was grown, no trace of it has been found.

LONICERA PERICLYMENUM
HONEYSUCKLE

The flowers have a delicious honey-sweet smell, especially in the evening. Honeysuckle is known as the emblem of love and affection because it twines round other plants as Titania says in Shakespeare's play *A Midsummer Night's Dream* when she is trying to bestow sleep upon Bottom:

'Sleep now, and I will wind thee in my arms, . . . so doth the woodbine, the sweet honeysuckle,
Gently entwine . . . . '

MELISSA OFFICINALIS
BALM

During Elizabethan times the stems were woven into garlands for their sweet fragrance, and the juice of balm was used to rub on to furniture to impart its lemon scent to the wood. The fresh leaves were placed in the bath to comfort and refresh the body. The lemon scented and flavoured leaves are much loved by bees (*melissa* is Greek for bee and *meli* means honey). Balm is also a pot-pourri herb.

MENTHA
MINTS

Members of the mint family are familiar to us as easily grown garden herbs with a pleasant aroma. All the mints yield fragrant oils. They were early strewing herbs and the leaves used to be placed in the bath both to scent it and to relax the muscles.

Mentha x piperata **Peppermint** oil is a useful flavouring in sweets, toothpaste and cosmetics.

Mentha dumetorum v. citrata is the beautifully scented **Eau-de-Cologne mint**.

Mentha spicata **Spearmint** This mint is used as a deodorant and its refreshing taste ensures its use in dental preparations.

Mentha suaveolens 'Variegata' **Pineapple Mint** is another delightfully scented mint.

Honeysuckle

MONARDA DIDYMA
BERGAMOT BEE BALM

The attractive red to purple flowers grow in whorls like a candelabra. The name comes from its perfume's similarity to the Bergamot orange. Its aromatic foliage is used to make bergamot oil and perfume.

MYRICA GALE
BOG-MYRTLE SWEET GALE

Bog-myrtle was used in Scotland as a domestic strewing herb on floors, to deter household pests, bugs and fleas and used for storing with linen, as a means of driving away moths and of scenting the cloth. The scent is improved when meadowsweet is added. The leaves of bog-myrtle emit a delightful perfume when touched; the wood is also scented. The berries, when treated with hot water, yield 'myrtle wax', a resinous substance with a powerful balsamic perfume. Candles made from this wax diffuse a delightful smell when burnt. The aromatic resins from the leaves give a peculiar flavour to milk when cows eat them.

NEPETA X FASSENII
GARDEN CATMINT

Catmints are popular ornamentals, with their aromatic soft blue-grey foliage and mauve flowers, suitable for edging herbaceous borders. Cats enjoy the plants either to chew the leaves or roll about on them in the heat of the summer. The constituent responsible for stimulating the cats is used in bait for trapping rodents.[4] The foliage of this hybrid catmint is strongly scented.

OCIMUM BASILICUM
BASIL

Basil is only half hardy in Britain but today as it is so readily available in pots for window-ledge growing it is rarely grown in the garden. The aromatic bright green leaves produce a scent with a clove-like fragrance, much loved by bees. Other varieties, especially the Greek basil, are becoming popular pot herbs. In France basil's essential oils are considered to be so similar to mignonette's scent that perfumiers blend them together.

OENOTHARA BIENNIS
EVENING-PRIMROSE

The flower 'sleeps' during the day and as twilight approaches the bloom opens to yield its scented beauty. It is powerfully fragrant at night, and is visited by night flying moths. The oil from the seeds which contains *gamma-linoleic* acid is used to soften and replenish dry skin. Increasing use of this herb may signal a time when we will see fields of these glorious yellow flowers.

ORIGANUM MARJORANA
SWEET MARJORAM

This is the most sweetly-scented of all the varieties of marjoram, and the most handsome. It was found in garlands on Egyptian mummies dating from the first century AD. Until the twentieth century its fragrance was considered to be one of the very finest coming only after rose, lavender and rosemary. It smells quite like thyme, although somewhat sweeter. Oil from the stems, leaves and seeds is used in food flavourings, perfumery, soaps and hair products.

PELARGONIUM
GERANIUM

This group of flowers must be considered to be among the best of all plants for window culture, always green, with varied leaf form and fragrance; try adding to pot pourris. The scented-leaved geraniums contain many volatile oils, some having a variety of perfumes. The most popular are the rose-scented ones like *Pelargonium* **Attar of Roses**; *Pelargonium crispum* when used fresh, gives a lemon flavour to sauces; *Pelargonium* **Prince of Orange** is one of the loveliest of the scented-leaved geraniums and smells refreshingly like orange while *Pelargonium tomentosum* smells of peppermint – a delicious 'peppermint' jelly is made from it. *Pelargonium vitifolium* has the scent of balm. Some are specifically grown to produce fragrant geranium oil, which is sometimes used as an adulterant in the manufacture of Attar of Roses perfume. *Pelargonium odoratissimum* has a most delightful scent of apples.

POPULUS X GILEADENSIS
BALM-OF-GILEAD

This is the true Balm-of-Gilead and the warm balsamic aroma is especially noticeable as the leaves unfold. The dried buds are added to pot pourris.

PRIMULA VERIS
COWSLIP

These used to be as abundant as buttercups, but over-picking and changes in farming practices have destroyed many of its habitats. They were once commonly used as cosmetics to enhance beauty and 'treat spots and wrinkles, sunburn and freckles'. (Culpepper, 1652)

ROSA
ROSES

Of all flowers roses possess a wider variety of perfume than any other species. The wild roses and the old shrub roses, being of purer breed than modern roses, possess a more distinctive perfume. Rose oil, or attar of roses, is a costly commodity, taking 1 ton of petals to produce 11oz of oil and for this reason much is synthetically produced. Some 96 per cent of women's perfumes contain rose oil.
Rosa alba is the white rose that was adopted by the **House of York** and has a very sweet smell. The double form is the symbol of our Royal Family.
Rosa alba maxima is the **Jacobite Rose**.
The **Red Rose of Lancaster** *Rosa gallica officinalis* has recently been planted along with *Rosa alba* for perhaps the first time since the Wars of the Roses in 1460, during London Garden Squares Day in London's Temple Gardens in an attempt to recreate a piece of history. The red and white varieties were famously plucked in the gardens by York and Lancastrian advers-aries at the start of the wars but the bushes had died out. But although the flowers are not as attractive as some modern roses it is of historic interest to see them growing together once again.

Burnet Rose

Eglantine

Rosa pimpinellifolia, the **Burnet Rose**, has the sweetest smell of any native rose – a mixture of honey and jasmine. As it blooms in the spring before other roses come into blossom; it is much valued; it is also extremely hardy. It is used therefore in rose breeding. Its double varieties are called the 'Scotch' roses.

Rosa eglanteria is the **Sweet Briar** or **Eglantine** and is also native. It has a delightful smell of apples, especially after rain – the scent coming from glands in the leaves. Its hybrid with the musk rose of the Himalaya is the only rose to give off its perfume from a distance.

Rosa damascena, one of the **Damask Roses**, was introduced very early probably by the Crusaders. It is one of the roses distilled to produce attar of roses. It is pale pink with a delicious sweet perfume and has been considered by one rose specialist to be one of the loveliest flowers in the world. Edward I was the first king to use it as his emblem.

One interesting variety that grows readily in Scotland is the **Bourbon rose 'Great Western'**, introduced in 1838 and named in honour of the famous steam and mail ship. It is a singularly beautiful variety producing an abundance of sumptuous large crimson-purple with a hint of maroon and is sweetly scented. It is a true cottage garden favourite as it roots readily from cuttings and thus commonly passed around! A beautiful specimen grows in the garden at Timespan in Helmsdale, Sutherland, suggesting that is hardy and very well worth considering.

ROSMARINUS OFFICINALIS
ROSEMARY

Rosemary is used in beauty preparations such as hair rinses – it conditions the hair and scalp. An infusion of rosemary mixed with a little borax, daily massaged into the scalp is said to be a good remedy for dandruff.[34] It is used also in bath oils etc. A volatile oil from the leaves forms an ingredient of Eau-de-Cologne. Bees love all varieties of rosemary. In olden days Greek scholars wore garlands of sweet-smelling rosemary when sitting examinations as they thought it might improve their memory and concentration.

SALVIA ELEGANS
'SCARLET PINEAPPLE'
PINEAPPLE SAGE

This aromatic and colourful herb is worth growing in any herb garden for a bit of extra colour and smell. Other sages are rich in volatile oils, which vary from species to species, producing a wide range of aromas, again invaluable in any herb garden.

SAMBUCUS NIGRA
ELDER

Elder-flower water makes a good skin tonic. In the Highlands the flowers were boiled in almond oil and lard, which gave a cream which was good for chapped skin and eczema, but should not be used for cuts or wounds.[5]

A Garden of Herbs

SAPONARIA OFFICINALIS
SOAPWORT
The two garden forms of soapwort are a double white and a double pink form and they look like large beautiful carnations. Both are sweetly scented. When the leaves are crushed and rubbed by the hands a lather-like soap is formed hence the name. The vegetable *saponins* that are produced from soapwort are so much more gentle than other *saponins* that they are made into fine soaps for washing valuable silks and ancient tapestries and to bring up the colour in antique materials.

SATUREJA MONTANA & HORTENSIS
WINTER & SUMMER SAVORY
Both of these Mediterranean plants were introduced to Britain, although the annual summer savory is more commonly grown. Winter savory has recently become naturalized, perhaps because the climate here is becoming warmer. John Josselyn, one of the early settlers in America, listed the savories as two of the plants introduced by them to remind them of the gardens they had left behind. Both species were noted by Virgil, in a poem, as being among the most fragrant of herbs and he also said that they should be planted near bee-hives.[24]

SENECIO JACOBAEA
RAGWORT
The vernacular name, Stinking Willie, comes from the stench of the leaves when crushed. It is believed that the 'Willie' referred to here is William ('The Butcher') Duke of Cumberland, who suppressed the Jacobite Rebellion on Culloden Moor, 1746.[26] Ragwort was apparently spread around by his forage in the campaign. After the Battle of Culloden in 1746 the victorious English are said to have renamed an attractive garden flower as Sweet William, in honour of their leader, the same William. The defeated Jacobites retaliated by naming the obnoxious weed Stinking Willy.[26] It is sometimes eaten by animals and is responsible for many cases of farm animal deaths.[39] According to oral tradition[48] it used to be put into the base of cornstacks to deter rats.

Soapwort

TANACETUM BALSAMITA
COSTMARY
Costmary has camphor scented foliage that can be dried to deter moths and used in pot pourri. The leaves of costmary have a balsamic scent when pressed and they are used in perfumery.

THYMUS
THYMES
All the thymes have aromatic foliage, each having a different scent. Some can be trodden upon and crushed producing a fragrant lawn, or make delight-ful garden plants growing among paving stones. Other thymes form miniature shrubs whose leaves and flowers attract many bees.
Thymus x citriodorus **Lemon Thyme** is a lemon-scented thyme. Variety *aureus* is the popular **Golden Thyme**.
Thymus vulgaris **Garden Thyme**

– in the Highlands where lavender does not grow well, sprigs of this and other thymes, are often used to scent handkerchiefs and linen.

URTICA DIOICA
COMMON NETTLE

Cloth made from nettles was made in Scotland as late as the nineteenth century. Nettle sheets and tablecloths were praised for combining fineness with strength. Nettle extracts contain a volatile oil, which has long been used in Europe as a hair rinse. The root has been an ingredient of some commercial hair growth preparations.[34]

VALERIANA OFFICINALIS
COMMON VALERIAN

A decoction of the aromatic root (really an underground stem) can be used as a soothing facial wash or for acne, and to scent linen. The flowers have a vanilla-like perfume but also contain valeric acid that is present in perspiration, hence sometimes one detects an unpleasant smell.

VIOLA ODORATA
SWEET VIOLET

The fragrance of this is very strong and was used to make perfume as far back as Classical Greek times. It was then in commercial cultivation for its sweetening properties and was so highly regarded that it became the symbol of ancient Athens. In Medieval Britain it was one of the strewing herbs.[39] Shakespeare appeared to have loved all scented plants: they are mentioned so often in his poetry. Violets he mentions in a number of his poems both as a fragrant flower and as one of the first flowers of the spring. In France vast numbers of violets are grown, not only for sale as posy bunches, but for the perfume industry.

Notes

Page 84 * Polunin, O & Huxley, A. (1965) *The Flowers of the Mediterranean* Chatto

Principle books and articles consulted

Genders[18] and Genders[19] comprehensive books on scented flowers;

Manniche[41] matters relating to early Egyptian, Greek and Roman uses of herbs;

The School of Scottish Studies[48] oral history;

The Illustrated Encyclopedia of Roses (1997) ed. Moody, M. beautifully illustrated comprehensive book on roses.

A Garden of Herbs

4.

Plants Used in Dyeing

We do not know what our ancestors used for dyes or how they knew how to achieve beautiful colours. Dyeing with natural products is a prehistoric craft although the first dyes were probably no more than fugitive stains obtained from fruit juices, flowers and decoctions of leaves, bark and roots.

Some of the dye plants of the ancient world were described by the Roman Pliny and the Greek Dioscorides. The earliest known fast dye, recorded from about 1727BC, and mentioned by Pliny, was extracted from an insect, *Kermes ilicis* and gave a beautiful red colour. The word crimson, which best describes the colour, comes from the word *kermes*. The first find of actual fabric treated with a fast and brilliant dye was in the excavation of a Greek tomb, and was a fragment of a purple robe. This brilliantly coloured dye was extracted from whelks (shellfish) and was mentioned in texts dating from about 1600BC. The dye was a major item of commerce for the Phoenicians who developed it and the purple was called Royal or Tyrian purple, because it originated in the city of Tyre, was prized above all other colours and was reserved strictly for the highest ranks in society. Because it was very costly and in great demand, a lichen growing near the sea was often used to dilute the colour. With the decline of the Roman Empire its use fell away and it was replaced by cheaper dyes which Dioscorides described: madder for red, saffron and weld for yellow, woad for blue and many others.

It is evident from their writings that the Romans already knew of the fast plant dye indigo, which came from the Orient. Pliny also recorded that wool to be dyed had to be first washed with soapwort, (*see Saponaria* in Aromatic section) and that alum was used as a fixative (a mordant) as it is today.

A Greek book of the third century, now in the Stockholm museum, gives many dye recipes. Excavations at Pompeii show how complete their dyers' workshops were. From the information in this dye book and from the dyers' workshop it seems that the perfection these early people may have attained with their primitive equipment could scarcely be outdone today. Many of the colours that were used have been described by Ovid in his *Art of Love*, where he advises women on the colours they should wear, such as 'pure blue of the cloudless sky'.

By the eighth century, merchants from every oriental city had headquarters at Damascus. Constantinople was even better able to link the business interests of East and West. European dyers in cities like Venice, a strategic location for trade, and Florence and other Mediterranean cities, were already flourishing in the tenth century and gained particular prominence by the thirteenth century. Dyers' guilds were established to exercise vigilance over maintaining a high standard. Later France became a centre of the dyeing trade and now native plants, such as woad, began to be used. Documents of 1361 tell of dyers travelling from many countries to a fair at Geneva to buy saffron, woad and alum (for use as a mordant) and other dye plants.[49]

Many wild plants have been used in Scotland for dyeing but it has not always been easy to distinguish them from other local plants in archaeological deposits. Some of the most significant information about dyeing comes from the excavation of a twelfth century archaeological site at Perth, where a concentration of possible dye plants, including seeds of dyer's rocket and tormentil were found, along with alpine and stag's-horn clubmoss. These clubmosses would not have been local to the area, so must have been brought there. It was not until the nineteenth century that these clubmosses were recognised as fixatives but this evidence does suggests a dyers' workshop.[14]

By the twelfth century Scotland's dyers' trade was regulated by law under David I (1124-1153). In England dyeing grew in importance by the fourteenth century as textile manufacture began to develop. Little is known, however, about the dyeing processes in Scotland before the seventeenth century. At this time fabric made from wool became more common than linen. Linen does not readily take up plant dyes, even with a mordant, although it will dye blue with woad or madder; silk was originally imported already dyed.[49]

Most traditional dye plants go straight into the pot with the wool (though tougher roots and bark are crushed or chopped, then strained). The type of pot used to prepare the dye turned out to be important. For example, wool dyed in an iron pot was found to give a different colour from that prepared in a copper one. The length of time of boiling and the use of different mordants also proved to be important. Copperas (ferrous sulphate), chrome, cream of tartar or a handful of coins were all tried out as fixatives and gave a range of colours even with the same dyestuff. The exact dyeing methods were carefully guarded secrets, hence very few were handed down. It was a form of self-expression, enabling women to dress their families a little bit differently from their neighbours.[5]

The most common mordant in the islands was urine (which gives off ammonia); the 'pee-tub' being a common sight outside every house. It was considered courteous to use the pot when visiting. Pee-pots were also found outside fulling (cleaning and shrinking) establishments in ancient Rome. Cloth was trodden underfoot in the stale urine mixed with water and Fuller's Earth. This was regularly used for cleaning the Romans' togas. The characteristic smell of true Harris Tweed is said to be of wool, dyestuff and urine! In fact, the smell comes from the lichen used in the dyeing, and not from urine.

In the past plants were often dug up in order to use their roots. Today this is not permitted. Unless plants have been grown specifically on one's own land for this purpose, roots must not be used. A plant whose roots were often used in the past for dyeing was Lady's bedstraw; the roots being traditionally dug up from the dunes and machair in summer, thereby causing much erosion. An Act of Parliament, passed in 1695, prohibited this destruction. However, the beauty of the red dye produced from this plant, coupled with its rarity, led to many clandestine night raids.

Lichens grow well in the warm wet West of Scotland, so they were also traditionally used – often in dyeing tweeds and tartans. Some of these lichens, such as crottle, lungwort and especially cudbear were of great economic significance, especially in dyeing Harris tweeds and kilt material. Recent research has shown that fungi also can be used in dyeing. Fungi, such as some of the *Pholiotas*, which give strong orange or moss green colours, depending on the mordant used, can produce a wide range of very fast dyes.

The great advances in dyeing methods began in France in

the eighteenth century when a dye chemistry, based on scientific principles, was developed. Natural dyes were universally used until the late 1880s when aniline dyes began to appear. Commercially, these replaced the plant dyes because they gave fast reproducible colours. Not until the mid- eighteenth century were imported dyes widely used in Scotland. A dye, called Turkey Red, produced in the Orient from madder, by a long-kept secret process, and which gave a very fast dye, arrived in Europe in 1747. A factory was set up on the Clyde at Glasgow by a French dyer in collaboration with David Dale in 1785.* Millions of yards of madder-dyed 'Turkey Red' cotton were later produced each year in the larger factory in the Vale of Leven, which closed only in 1960.

The discovery of synthetic aniline dyes (derived from coal tar) at the end of the 1880s, which give stronger and more reliable matching, led to the decline of dyeing with plants. Today, however, plants are being used once again to create some of the traditional softer shades, rather than the harsher ones produced by chemical dyes.

Plant name	Part used	Mordant	Comment
YELLOW/ GREEN COLOURS			
Agrimonia eupatoria **Agrimony**	flowering tops	alum	beautiful golden yellow
Anthemis tinctoria **Yellow Chamomile**		chrome	strong yellow
Betula species **Birch**	leaves	alum	lemon yellow
Calendula officinalis **Pot Marigold**	flowers		boil; bright yellow flowers are best
Calluna vulgaris **Heather/Ling**	flowers	alum	yellow, gold, green
Digitalis purpurea **Foxglove**	leaves & inflorescence	alum & cream of tartar	information from a modern dyer, roots were once used as a mordant
Erica cinerea **Bell Heather**	flowers	alum	yellow, gold, green
Filipendula ulmaria **Meadowsweet**	flowers	alum copper	yellow, green, black depending on mordant lime-yellow
Fraxinus excelsior **Ash**	male & female flowers	alum & soda	linden green
Genista tinctoria **Dyer's Greenweed**	flowering tops	alum	signal yellow

A Garden of Herbs

Plant name	Part used	Mordant	Comment
Hypericum perforatum **St John's-wort**	flowers	alum	yellow, green, black, maroon in a single dye bath
Iris pseudacorus **Yellow Iris**	leaves	alum	modern dyers get pale yellow
Malus sylvestris **Crab Apple**	bark	alum	yellow
Mentha **Mints**	flowering tops	alum	yellow, olive
Myrica gale **Bog-myrtle**	leaves	alum	very good signal yellow
		iron sulphate	green; tin gives a yellow-green
Persicaria maculosa **Redshank**	whole plant	alum	yellow, intense green
Pteridium aquilinum **Bracken**	roots	chrome	yellow
Pulmonaria officinalis **Lungwort**	whole plant	alum	intense green/yellow with ammonia added
Reseda luteola **Weld**	tops & flowers	soda	primary yellow, grows in Scotland but was long imported
Rubus idaeus **Raspberry**	leaves	alum	fruits do not give fast colour
Sambucus nigra **Elder**	leaves	alum	'Genet' yellow; olive with iron
Senecio jacobaea **Ragwort**	flowering tops	iron sulphate	dull green
		copper sulphate	golden olive
Tanacetum vulgare **Tansy**	flowering tops	alum	intense yellow
Ulex europaeus **Gorse**	flowers	alum	'Genet' yellow, olive
Urtica dioica **Nettle**	whole tops	alum	olive-yellow

RED/ BROWN COLOURS

Anchusa officinalis **Alkanet**	roots		red
Betula species **Birch**	bark	alum	cardinal red, caramel, brownish orange
Erica cinerea **Bell Heather**	stalks & tops	alum	brownish orange
Filipendula ulmaria **Meadowsweet**	roots	ferrous sulphate	raw umber, black with iron
Galium verum **Lady's Bedstraw**	roots	alum	cardinal red
Humulus lupulus **Hop**	vine and fruit	alum	brownish tomato red

Plant name	Part used	Mordant	Comment
Iris pseudacorus **Yellow Iris (Flag)**	roots	iron	burnt umber
	ripe seeds	tin or none	bright red-brown or burnt sienna depending on mordant
Lobaria pulmonaria **Lungwort**	whole lichen	none	burnt sienna, terracotta
Malus sylvestris **Crab Apple**	young bark	alum	golden yellow, orange yellow,
	mature leaves	alum	orange yellow or burnt umber depending on mordant
Origanum vulgare **Wild Marjoram**	flowering tops	malt & yeast tin	red, also gold and brown 'Turkey Red'
Potentilla erecta **Tormentil**	rhizome	alum plus soda pre-mordant with iron	greyish-orange violet-brown
Prunus avium **Gean**	frosted leaves	iron	burnt umber, golden brown, khaki
Rubia tinctorum **Madder**	powdered roots	alum	'Turkey Red', although growing in Britain it was imported into Scotland from the 11th century
Rumex acetosa **Sorrel**	roots	alum	brick red, burnt sienna
Rumex obtusifolius **Broad-leaved Dock**	ripe seeds	alum	various reds – amber, caramel, garnet brown
Rumex crispus **Curled Dock**	ripe seeds	alum	'Venetian Red'
Salix species **Willows**	stems & leaves	alum	signal yellow, burnt sienna, dark brown, nearly black

PURPLE/BLUE COLOURS

Plant name	Part used	Mordant	Comment
Empetrum nigrum **Crowberry**	ripe berries	alum	delft blue, dyes linen very well, most berry dyes fade in sunlight
Indigofera tinctoria **Indigo**			blue, the most successful imported early dyestuff
Isatis tinctoria **Woad**	first year leaves	washing-soda	deep blue, very important early dye
Ochrolechia tartarea **Cudbear**	whole lichen		significant from 1750-1950 in Britain, recorded 1st century by Pliny

A Garden of Herbs

Plant name	Part used	Mordant	Comment
Sambucus nigra **Elder**	berries & leaves	iron sulphate	violet & oriental blue
Taraxicum species **Dandelion**	root		magenta with wool
Vaccinium myrtillus **Blaeberry**	ripe berries	iron, alum	much used because of scarcity of blue dyes, but not fast
BLACK/GREY COLOURS			
Alnus glutinosa **Alder**	bark	ferrous sulphate	black
Angelica sylvestris **Angelica**	roots	ferrous sulphate	charcoal black
Arctostaphylos uva-ursi **Bearberry**	leaves	ferrous sulphate	charcoal black
Crataegus monogyna **Hawthorn**	bark	alum	bark boiled, soaked then strained, many tree barks give a black dye
Filipendula ulmaria **Meadowsweet**	flowering tops	ferrous sulphate	good deep black
Iris pseudacorus **Yellow Iris**	roots	iron	black
Nymphaea alba **White Water-lily**	rhizome	copperas	black

Several plants in these tables will not be in many herb gardens but have been such important dye plants in Scotland that they have been included.

Principle books or articles consulted

Greirson[25] an excellent book, very well researched but difficult to obtain;
MacIntyre[37] also well researched but difficult to obtain;
Schetky [37] this mainly historical booklet I found to be fascinating;
Fraser, J. (1996) *Traditional Scottish Dyes* Canongate – is more easily obtainable.

List is based on Ross (1895)[47] 'as complete a list of native plants used for dyes as I have been able to procure'.

Colour	Plant used	Latin name
Black	Flag Iris root	*Iris pseudacorus*
	Alder (with copperas)	*Alnus glutinosa*
	Dock root	*Rumex species*
	Oak bark and acorns	*Quercus species*
Brown	Crottle	*Parmelia saxatilis*
	Yellow Wall Lichen	*Parmelia parietina*
	Dark Crottle	*P. ceratophylla*
	Dulse (Seaweed)	*Rhodymenia edulis*
Dark Brown	Blaeberry with nut galls	*Vaccinium myrtillus*
	Redcurrant (with alum)	*Ribes rubrum*
	Water Lily root	*Nymphaea alba*
Faun	Birch bark	*Betula species*
Blue	Blaeberry (with copperas)	*Vaccinium myrtillus*
	Elder (with alum)	*Sambucus nigra*
Blue-black	Sloe	*Prunus spinosa*
	Red Bearberry	*Arctostaphyllus uva-ursi*
Dark green	Heath (pulled just before flowering from a dark shady place)	*Erica cinerea*
	Gorse/ Whin (bark)	*Ulex europaea*
Green	Flag Iris leaf	*Iris pseudachorus*
Bright green	Weld (with indigo)	*Resida luteola*
Purple	Blaeberry (with alum)	*Vaccinium myrtillus*
	Sundew	*Drossera rotundifolia*
Violet	Water Cress	*Rorippa nasturtium-aquaticum*
	Vetch	*Vicia orobus (not common in Scotland)*
Red	Rock Lichen (Crotal)	*Ramalina scopulorum*
	Crotal Gael	*Lecanora pallescens*
	Blaeberry	*Vaccinium myrtillus*
	(with verdigris and ammonia)	

Bright red	Lady's Bedstraw	*Galium verum*
	Tormentil	*Potentilla erecta*
Scarlet	Crotal corkir (ground and mixed with urine)	*Lecanora tartarea*
	Limestone Lichen	*Urcelaria calcarea*
Yellow	Crab Apple	*Malus sylvestris*
	Ash	*Fraxinus excelsior*
	Ash root	
	Aspen	*Populus tremula*
	Elm	*Ulmus glabra*
	Bog Myrtle	*Myrica gale*
	Bracken root	*Pteridium aquilinum*
Bright yellow	St John's Wort	*Hypericum perforatum*
	Sundew (with ammonia)	*Drosera rotundifolia*
Orange	Ragwort (Stinking Willie)	*Senecio jacobea*
	Barbery root	*Berberis vulgaris*
Dark orange	Bramble	*Rubus fruticosa*
Magenta	Dandelion	*Taraxicum species*

Plant Badges of the Clans

The plant badge of a clansman was a sprig fixed on a staff, spear or bonnet. Obviously incapable of being a distinguishing emblem there is ground for believing that it was the clan's charm-plant like an amulet or talisman.

The Scottish Tartans (1999) revised by Sir Thomas Innes of Learney, pub. Johnston & Bacon, Stirling

Brodie	Periwinkle
Bruce	Rosemary
Buchanan	Blaeberry, Birch
Cameron	Crowberry, Cranberry, Oak
Campbell	Myrtle (?Bog Myrtle)
Chisholm	Fern
Colquhoun	Hazel
Davidson	Red Whortleberry
Drummond	Holly
Farquharson	Scots 'Fir' (Pine)
Fergusson	Poplar
Forbes	Broom
Fraser	Yew
Gordon	Ivy
Grant	Scots Pine
Gunn	Juniper, Rose
Hamilton	Bay
Henderson	Cotton Grass
Innes	Great Bulrush
Kennedy	Oak
Leslie	Rue (? Meadow Rue)
Macalister	Ling, Heather
Macalpine	Scots Pine
Macarthur	Wild Thyme
Macdonald	Heather
Macdougall	Bell Heather
Macfarlane	Cloudberry, Cranberry
MacGillivray	Red Whortlebeerry
Macgregor	Scots Pine
Macintosh	Bearberry, Cowberry
Macintyre	Heather, White Heather
Mackay	Great Bulrush
Mackenzie	Deer Grass
Mackinnon	St John's-wort
Maclachlan	Rowan
Maclean	Crowberry
Maclennan	Gorse
Macleod	Juniper, Red Whortleberry
Macmillan	Holly
Macnaughton	Trailing Azelea
Macneil	Dryas (Mountain Avens)
Macnicol	Juniper, Trailing Azelea
Macpherson	White Heather
Malcolm	Rowan berries
Mathieson	Four petal Rose
Menzies	Menzies Heath
Morrison	Driftweed
Munro	Common Clubmoss
Murray	Juniper
Ogilvy	Alkanet, Hawthorn
Robertson	Bracken
Ross	Juniper
Scott	Blaeberry
Stewart	Oak
Sutherland	Common Sedge
Urquart	Wallflower

5.
The Highland
Scottish medical tradition

An important phase of early Scottish medicine is found in Gaelic Medieval Manuscripts, preserved in several major libraries, the largest number being in the National Library of Scotland. Several are based on authoritative treatises by Hippocrates, Galen (*c*.150AD), Pliny and also the Arab physician Avicenna (*c*.1000AD) whose names are cited in the manuscripts. Sadly only one of these important manuscripts has been translated from the Gaelic.

Some Scottish physicians may even have studied at the Monastery of Monte Cassino, founded in 529AD,* 'where monks from fringe lands came for instruction',[2] or at the medical school at Salerno which became famous in the eleventh century. This school had its own Rule of Health, *Regimen Sanitatis*,[4] which was translated into Gaelic, in the late fourteenth or early fifteenth century by John MacBeath. It became the bible of medical health in Highland Scotland, and copies were often annotated with information they already knew or had learned by experience. For example, James Beaton of Mull wrote in the margin of one of the manuscripts he carried around with him, opposite the herb betony, that he regularly used this herb, also noting that according to other medieval manuscripts it was much used.

It is known that many Scots studied at the medical school at Montpellier, founded *c*1137AD. A Scot, by the name of Bernard Gordon, was a professor there and he wrote *Lilium Medicinae*, which was issued in the year 1305. The MacBeaths possessed a copy of this and treated it with the greatest care. On one occasion, when visiting a patient, because the doctor had to travel across a loch by boat, the precious manuscript was carried by the longer journey round the loch. It was a well respected textbook during the Middle Ages. Other hereditary physicians such as the MacConachers of Argyll also practised but the MacBeaths, or Beatons as they later came to be called (or Macbeths, MacBeads, Bethunes, etc which are all forms of the same Gaelic name), were the most respected and influential of the medical dynasties in the Highlands. The Highland Scottish medical profession was well-organised and physicians were practising medicine long before the 'Islamic varieties came to Europe as law tracts of the seventh and eighth centuries testify'.*

Learning was much esteemed and was fostered by the clan chiefs in the Highlands, such as the Lords of the Isles, who established a medical service in many parts of their widely scattered lands. The name MacBeath occurs in the Scottish Book of Deer, inserted between the dates 900 and 1100 where it also says that Alexander I created a certain Donald MacBead as governor of the castle in Dingwall in 1110. Tradition has it that every monarch from David I (1124 -1153), to King James VI (1567-1625) had a Beaton doctor. James even took his physician with him to the court in London. It is recorded that during the reign of Robert II (1371-1390), one of the Beatons, by virtue of being a physician, was given a grant of land by the Wolf of Badenoch. The Beatons practised over a large part of Scotland and enjoyed patronage of noble families from the latter half of the fourteenth to the eighteenth century.

The medical doctors in Scotland had privileges similar to nobles by virtue of their skills, and had a high place in the hierarchy of the clan, coming second only to the bard at banquets.[2] Professors of Medicine enjoyed a title equal to that of Earls. They married women from noble families and travelled widely in Europe: many went to the universities of Montpellier and Bologna and later to Leyden. It is of interest that Cardinal Beaton belonged to this family.

What is most notable in the medical advice given in *Regimen Sanitatus* is the emphasis on common sense and healthy living in the prevention of disease. In the view of the physicians the mind played an important role in determining the state of bodily health. 'Cast from you heavy wories and be convinced that it will not profit you to be angry', 'keep a firm grip on health'. Diet was equally important, 'do not eat too much', 'eat to live not live to eat', 'if you wish to be light let your supper be short'.

They discussed what constitutes a good and healthy daily

routine. On rising in the morning exercise was recommended, with 'moderate walking in high clean places', although not immediately after a meal, as 'too great excercise after a meal interferes with digestion'. It was suggested that after breakfast a man should 'expel the superfluities of the first digestion'. (regularity in all things!)

Cleanliness and personal hygiene were believed to be very important. People were told to put on clean clothes and to 'comb his hair and wash his hands and rub his nec', then 'rub his teeth with the skin of a yellow apple' and 'wash his eyes with water which has been held in his own mouth and warmed' and told that for drinking, 'water must be clean'. It is of considerable interest to me that my father, a MacDonald from North Uist related to me many of these words of wisdom, and encouraged me to clean my teeth with apples.

Food and its preparation were discussed at length, and even invalid diets were considered. Their comments on food are interesting; 'the time to eat fruit is after other food', 'nuts are always healthy for the livers'. They had quite a lot to say about who should benefit from a spot of wine. First they said, 'spare the wine'. However they went on to recommend that 'a little wine may give comfort to the old men', 'give it in the quantity they wish . . . indeed they ought to have it in good quantity', but 'give it in moderation to the young men'!

One particular treatment and diet was prescribed for a patient suffering from a wound. According to advice given in *Lilium Medicinae,* wounds should be kept 'open' during the treatment.

> 'Let the food be tender and let him partake of gruel or
> barley-water and the wine of pomegranate as a drink and
> let him take soup made with almonds as a diet and let
> him take spinach and beetroot and borage and lettuce
> and others like them, and let him continue that diet until
> the wound festers, and, after that when matter begins to
> develop in it since thereby the patient is weakened give
> him the flesh of kids or chickens boiled in water and give
> him soup mixed with the yolk of an egg . . . and have no
> fear, for nature herself will cure him'.[4]

With good cooking methods, *eg* 'Roast things kept overnight are not good, even if a covering is upon them' and cleanliness was recommended. Thus food poisoning was probably avoided.

The physicians added to the teachings contained in these two important manuscripts their own store of native medical knowledge, which was purely herbal in character. 'There is much talk of botany, particularly of the medicinal, food value, and toxic properties of plants'. Extracts of simple herbs are prescribed: 'violet for headache & catarrh; nettle, mustard, hyssop and shepherd's purse for bleeding wounds; fennel and parsley to increase urine flow; celery for diseases of the mouth and stomach; mercury for lice; tannins for wounds'.

There was a highly regarded herb garden at Pennycross on Mull, which can still be traced, where one of the Beatons lived around 1594. There is no record of the herbs that were grown there, but there are records of the herbs grown at the Edinburgh herb garden, founded in 1681, which, it was said, grew the same herbs, and we know that they grew over eight hundred different varieties.

The Highland physicians seem to have have had some reservations regarding blood-letting, which was a fashionable treatment in other parts of the country for centuries, and which often did more harm than good. They recommended that it 'should not be over-practiced', and only practised if at the right time and conditions. Warnings are given against the danger of over-doing it, *eg* 'Only a young man and he is resting and using of flesh of red meat and other food which nourishes well, will benefit from this.'

There are some amusing stories told about one of the Beatons, which record his skill. The King's physicians were jealous of their ability so on one occasion decided to thwart the doctor in his diagnosis, and substituted urine from a cow in place of the King's urine. After a careful examination of the patient and of 'his' urine, Beaton addressed them saying, 'If you gentlemen open up His Majesty, you will find him to be in calf'. He then went on to treat the King who, it is recorded, did recover.

Martin,[42] a graduate in medicine from Leyden University who travelled widely in the Highlands, reported that the success attending one of the Beatons, who lived at his own time, was so extraordinary that people thought his cures came from a pact with the devil rather than from his knowledge of herbs. Many members of this family were famous all over the country and had much success in treating many diseases.

The Lowland medical tradition

Small hospitals, many attached to religious houses, were common in Lowland Scotland from Anglo-Saxon times but collection of revenues was always a problem and as the church became more and more corrupt towards the Reformation revenues originally intended for the upkeep of the hospitals and support of the poor were used by churchmen. One of the things Knox did after the Reformation was to produce a plan for social welfare and this included medical education.*

Families practising medicine on a hereditary basis were not confined to Gaelic-speaking Scotland, but they were much less common and not so highly respected. One of the main differences between Highland and Lowland medical practice in the Middle Ages was that surgeons and barber-surgeons (who occupied a rather lowly position) became more powerful earlier than physicians in the Lowlands, and many were not well qualified. This had important effects. People were reluctant to go for treatment. The doctors also depended mainly on the Latin texts, like their counterparts in England, whereas the Gaelic physicians, who were wealthy, well-educated men had Greek and Arabic as well as the Latin texts to which they had added their own native learning.

Gaelic medical manuscripts that had been used in the Highlands outnumber the Latin manuscripts preserved in Lowland Scotland, many of which must have been lost during the Reformation. There were a few learned men, like Michael Scot, who practised medicine and while he used herbs in some of his treatments he charged exorbitant sums of money, well over £3000 sterling, in today's currency, for treating a few important patients.** In the Lowlands, herbal remedies would not necessarily be people's first choice. People believed in the power of healing stones and holy healing wells, such as St Columba's Well. Prayer and pilgrimage to Scotland's holy places, such as Whithorn, where St Ninian's relics were to be found, were thought to produce cures.

There must also have been a network of local folk healers,

bonesetters and travelling honest and dishonest healers. In the 1599 Charter to the Faculty of Physicians and Surgeons in Glasgow, there is a complaint against '. . . ignorant unskillit and unlernit personis quha. . . abuses the people'.

The use of herbs must have become more acceptable as by the sixteenth century (c.1555) we know of at least one herb garden, probably attached to Glasgow Cathedral, about which the physician Mark Jameson wrote. He left a list of herbs, some culinary but mainly strongly medicinal/gynaecological.[15] A garden commemorating Mark Jameson's contribution to medical history has recently been opened at the University of Glasgow. In addition a book giving information about medical plants, first published in Germany, was sold in Glasgow in 1549 and in 1627 a mail-order drug catalogue promoting the sale of herbs was published in Aberdeen. This was the *Pharmacopinax* of William Garden.

In Edinburgh, the Royal College of Physicians, concerned with the poor quality of drugs being dispensed,* obtained powers to visit apothecaries' shops, but with the establishment of the Edinburgh Physic garden in 1681 fresh herbs were available. Methods of dispensing were regulated and given in two different *Pharmacopaeia*. The earliest, *Pharmacopaeia Edinburgensis Pauperum* (1683), mentions over eight hundred herbs, including valerian, angelica, horse-radish and more exotic plants such as palm oil, lemons, nutmegs and even French brandy and Canary wine. These latter were recommended to be taken with opium, presumably used by surgeons to dull the pain of operations.

It is sad that the long tradition of the medical dynasties of the Highlands and Islands, where knowledge was handed down from one generation to the next, has ended. This was probably inevitable with changes in the way medicine is studied in modern times. What is serious is the loss of knowledge of how to use herbs, held by people of the generation of my parents. The social and political upheavals of the nineteenth century which forced people to leave their homes and find work in the cities must have had an effect in this process. The introducton of Medical Officers of Health to the Highlands and Islands may have undermined people's confidence in their own medical traditions. The introduction of sheep had a devastating effect on the numbers of herbs growing wild which must have made collection of these more difficult.

A Garden of Herbs

In more recent years, however, there has been a resurgence of interest in culinary and medical herbs, partly encouraged by commercial interests, but largely stimulated by collectors of traditions such as the School of Scottish Studies of Edinburgh University, or independent scholars. Dr Margaret Fay Shaw Campbell,[50] has written about traditional herbs from South Uist, and Mary Beith[5] with her regular articles in the *West Highland Free Press* has encouraged the beginning of a real interest in herbs that have been used and valued for many centuries.

Notes

Page 101 * Rashdall, H, ed. & Rev Powicke, FM & Emden, AB (1936) *The Universities of Europe in the Middle Ages* Clarenden Press, Oxford

Page 102* Fleetwood, J (1951) *History of Medicine in Ireland* Brown & Nolan

Page 105* Comrie, JD (1932) *History of Scottish Medicine* Vol I, The Wellcome History of Medicine Museum

Page 105 ** Hamilton, D (1981) *The Healers: a History of Medicine in Scotland* Canongate, Edinburgh

Page 106 * Ritchie, RP (1899) *The Early Days of The Royal Colledge of Physicians, Edinburgh* George & Johnston, Edinburgh

Principle books and texts consulted

Bannerman[2] information on the Beatons as a medical kindred in the classical Gaelic tradition;
Beaton[4] a translation into English from Gaelic of ancient Arabic texts on medical health;
Beith[5] Scottish/Highland history of uses, especially medical;
Dickson, J.H. & Gauld[15] a possible sixteenth century garden for gynaecology in Glasgow;
Martin[42] travels in the Western Isles of Scotland *circa* 1695;
Nicolson[45] the McBeths as hereditary physicians of the Highlands;
Pennant[4] description of travels in Scotland, 1779;
School of Scottish Studies[48] oral history often medical.

English / Latin

Absinthe	*Artemisia absinthium*
Agrimony	*Agrimonia eupatoria*
Alder	*Alnus glutinosa*
Alkanet	*Anchusa officinalis*
Aloe Vera	*Aloe vera*
Angelica, Garden	*Angelica archangelica*
Angelica, Wild	*Angelica sylvestris*
Apple, Crab	*Malus sylvestris*
Apple	*Malus domestica*
Artichoke, Globe	*Cynara cardunculus*
Ash	*Fraxinus excelsior*
Asparagus	*Asparagus officinalis*
Asthma Weed	*Euphorbia hirta*
Autumn Crocus	*Crocus sativus*
Baldmony	*Meun athamanticum*
Balm (Lemon)	*Melissa officinalis*
Balm, Golden	*Melissa officinalis 'Aurea'*
Balm-of-Gilead	*Populus* x *Gileadensis*
Balm-of-Gilead (false)	*Cedronella canariensis*
Baneberry	*Actaea spicata*
Barley	*Hordeum vulgare*
Basil	*Ocimum basillicum*
Bay, Sweet	*Laurus nobilis*
Bearberry	*Arctostaphyllus uva-ursi*
Bergamot	*Monarda didyma*
Bergamot, Lemon	*Monarda citriodora*
Betony	*Stachys officinalis*
Bilberry (Blaeberry)	*Vaccinium myrtillus*
Birch	*Betula*
Bishop's-weed	*Aegopodium podagraria*
Bistort	*Persicaria bistorta*
Bitter-vetch	*Lathyrus linifolius*
Blackcurrant	*Ribes nigrum*
Bog-bean	*Menyanthes trifoliata*
Bogmosses	*Sphagnum*
Bog-myrtle	*Myrica gale*
Boneset	*Eupatorium perfoliatum*

Borage	*Borago officinalis*
Box	*Buxus sempervirens*
Bracken	*Pteridium aquilinum*
Bramble	*Rubus fruticosus*
Broom	*Cytisus scoparius*
Bugle	*Ajuga reptans*
Burnet Rose	*Rosa pimpinellifolia*
Butcher's-broom	*Ruscus aculeatus*
Calamint	*Clinopodium officinalis*
Calamint, Greater	*Clinopdoium grandiflorum*
Camphor Plant	*Tanacetum balsamita v. balsamita*
Caraway	*Carum carvi*
Carrot, Wild	*Daucus carota*
Catmint, Garden	*Nepeta x fassenii*
Catmint, Wild	*Nepeta catariae*
Cat's Foot	*Anteneria dioica*
Celandine, Greater	*Chelidonium majus*
Celandine, Lesser	*Ranunculus ficaria*
Celery, Wild	*Apium graveolens*
Chamomile (Roman)	*Chamaemelum nobile*
Chamomile, Dyer's (Yellow)	*Anthemis tinctoria*
Chamomile, German	*Matricaria recutita*
Chamomile, Lawn	*C. nobile* 'Treneague'
Chamomile, Lemon	*Anthemis tinctoria*
Cherry, Bird	*Prunus padus*
Cherry, Wild or Gean	*Prunus avium*
Chervil, Garden	*Anthriscus cerefolium*
Chives	*Allium schoenoprassum*
Chives, Garlic	*Allium tuberosum*
Clary, Wild	*Salvia verbenaceae*
Clove Pink	*Dianthus caryophyllus*
Colt's-foot	*Tussilago farfara*
Columbine	*Aquilegia vulgaris*
Comfrey, Common	*Symphytum officinale*
Comfrey, Tuberous	*Symphytum tuberosum*
Coneflower	*Echinacea angustifolia*
Coriander	*Coriandrum sativum*
Costmary	*Tanacetum balsamita*
Cowberry	*Vaccinium vitis-idea*
Cowslip	*Primula veris*
Crab Apple	*Malus sylvestris*
Cranberry	*Vaccinium oxycocccus*
Cranberry, Large	*Vaccinium macrocarpus*
Crane's-bill, American	*Geranium maculatum*
Crane's-bill, Cut-leaved	*Geranium dissectum*
Crocus, Autumn	*Colchicum autumnale*
Crocus, Saffron	*Crocus sativus*
Crowberry	*Empetrum nigrum*
Cudbear	*Ochroleucia tartarea*

A Garden of Herbs

Cumin	*Cuminum cyminum*
Damask Rose	*Rosa damascena*
Dame's-violet	*Hesperis matronalis*
Dandelion	*Taraxacum offininale*
Deadly Nightshade	*Atropa belladonna*
Dill	*Anethum graveolens*
Dock, Broad-leaved	*Rumex obtusifolius*
Dock, Curled	*Rumex crispus*
Dyer's Chamomile	*Anthemis tinctoria*
Dyer's Greenweed	*Genista tinctoria*
Dyer's Knotweed	*Polygonum tinctoria*
Eglantine	*Rosa eglanteria*
Elder, Golden	*Sambucus nigra 'Aurea'*
Elder	*Sambucus nigra*
English Flag	*Achillea agaratum*
Evening-primrose	*Oenothera biennis*
Fennel	*Foeniculum vulgare*
Feverfew	*Tanacetum parthenium*
Flax, Cultivated	*Linum usitatissimum*
Foxglove	*Digitalis purpurea*
Garlic	*Allium sativum*
Garlic Chives	*Allium tuberosum*
Garlic, Wild	*Allium ursinum*
Gean	*Prunus avium*
Gean	*Prunus avium*
Geranium, scented	*Pelargonium*
Ginkgo	*Ginkgo biloba*
Ginseng, American	*Panax quinquefolius*
Ginseng, Chinese	*Panax ginseng*
Glasswort	*Salicornia europea*
Globe Artichoke	*Cynara cardunculus*
Goat's-rue	*Galega officinalis*
Good-King-Henry	*Chenopodium bonus-henricus*
Gorse	*Ulex europaeus*
Greater Celandine	*Chelidonium majus*
Ground-elder	*Aegopodium podagraria*
Hawthorn	*Crataegus monogyna*
Heather (Ling)	*Calluna vulgaris*
Heather, Bell	*Erica cinerea*
Hemlock	*Conium maculatum*
Hemlock Water-dropwort	*Oenanthe crocata*
Henbane	*Hyoscamus niger*
Holly	*Ilex aquifolium*
Holy Grass	*Hieriochloe odorata*
Honeysuckle	*Lonicera periclymenum*
Hop	*Humulus lupulus*
Hop, Fuggle	*Humulus lupulus 'Fuggle'*
Horse-radish	*Armoracia rusticana*
Hyssop	*Hyssopus officinalis*

Hyssop, Anise	*Agastache foeniculum*
Indigo	*Indigofera tinctoria*
Iris, Yellow (Yellow Flag)	*Iris pseudacorus*
Ivy	*Hedera helix*
Juniper	*Juniperous communis*
Lady's Bedstraw	*Galium verum*
Lady's-mantle	*Alchemilla vulgaris*
Lavender	*Lavandula officinalis*
Lavender, Cotton	*Santolina chamaecyparissus*
Lavender, English	*Lavandula angustifolia*
Lavender, Garden	*Lavandula x intermedia*
Lavender, Spike	*Lavandula latifolia*
Lesser Celendine	*Ranunculus ficaria*
Lily-of-the-valley	*Convallaria majalis*
Liquorice	*Glycyrrhiza glabra*
Lovage	*Levisticum officinale*
Lovage, Scots	*Ligusticum scoticu*
Love Parsley	*Levisticum officinale*
Lungwort (lichen)	*Lobaria pulmonaria*
Lungwort	*Pulmonaria officinalis*
Mace, English	*Achillea ageratum*
Madder	*Rubia tinctorum*
Magnolia	*Magnolia officinalis*
Male Fern	*Dryopteris filix-mas*
Mallow, Common	*Malva sylvestris*
Mandrake	*Mandragora officinarum*
Marigold, Pot	*Calendula officinalis*
Marjoram, Pot	*Origanum onites*
Marjoram, Sweet	*Origanum marjorana*
Marjoram, Wild	*Origanum vulgare*
Marsh Marigold	*Caltha palustris*
Marsh-mallow	*Althaea officinalis*
Mayweed, Scented	*Matricaria recutita*
Meadow Saffron	*Colchicum autumnale*
Meadowsweet	*Filipendula ulmaria*
Mezereon	*Daphne mezereum*
Milk Thistle	*Silybum marianum*
Mint family	*Mentha* family
Apple-mint	*M. x villosa*
Bowles' Mint	*M. x villosa v. alopecuroides*
Corsican Mint	*M. requienii*
Eau de Cologne Mint	*M.dumetorum v. citrata*
Morocan Mint	*M. x smithiana* 'Moroccan'
Pennyroyal	*M. pulegium*
Peppermint	*M. x piperata*
Pineapple Mint	*M. suaveolins 'variegata'*
Red Raripala Mint	*M. x smithiana*
Spear Mint	*M. spicata*
Monk's-hood	*Aconitum napellus*

A Garden of Herbs

Mountain Everlasting	*Anteneria dioica*
Mugwort	*Artemisia vulgaris*
Nasturtium	*Tropaeolum majus*
Nasturtium, Tuberous	*Tropaeolum tuberosum*
Nettle, Common	*Urtica dioica*
Onion	*Allium cepa*
Opium Poppy	*Papaver somniferum*
Oregano	*Origanum vulgare*
Orris	*Iris germanica* v. *florintina*
Parsley	*Petroselinum crispum*
Pasque Flower	*Pulsatilla vulgaris*
Periwinkle, Greater	*Vinca major*
Periwinkle, Lesser	*Vinca minor*
Periwinkle, Madagascar	*Catharanthus roseus*
Polypody	*Polypodium vulgare*
Poppy, Common	*Papaver rhoeas*
Poppy, Opium	*Papaver somniferum*
Primrose	*Primula vulgaris*
Ragwort	*Senecio jacobaea*
Ransomes	*Allium ursinum*
Raspberry	*Rubus idaeus*
Redshank	*Polygonum persicaria*
Rhubarb	*Rheum x hybridum*
Rock Samphire	*Crithmum maritimum*
Rocket	*Eruca vesicaria* ssp. *sativa*
Rose, Burnet	*Rosa pimpinellifolia*
Rose, Damask	*Rosa damascena*
Rose, Eglantine	*Rosa eglanteria*
Rose, House of York	*Rosa alba*
Rosemary	*Rosmarinus officinalis*
Roseroot	*Sedum rosea*
Rowan	*Sorbus aucuparia*
Rue	*Ruta graveolens*
Saffron Crocus	*Crocus sativus*
Saffron, Meadow	*Colchicum autumnale*
Sage	*Salvia officinalis*
Sage, Golden	*Salvia officinalis 'Aurea'*
Sage, Jerusalem	*Phlomis fruticosa*
Sage, Pineapple	*S. elegans 'Scarlet Pineapple'*
Samphire, Rock	*Crithmum maritimimum*
Savory, Summer	*Satureja hortensis*
Savory, Winter	*Satureja montana*
Scurvy Grass	*Cochlearia officinalis*
Sea-buckthorn	*Hippophae rhamnoides*
Sea-holly	*Eryngium maritimum*
Seaweeds	*Algae*
Selfheal	*Prunella vulgaris*
Silverweed	*Potentilla anserina*
Snowdrop	*Galanthus nivalis*

Soapwort	*Saponaria officinalis*
Sorrel, Common	*Rumex acetosa*
Southernwood	*Artemisia abrotanum*
Sphagnum Bogmosses	*Sphagnum*
Spignel	*Meun athamanticum*
Spurge Olive	*Daphne mezereum*
St John's-wort	*Hypericum perfoliatum*
Strawberry, Wild	*Fragaria vesca*
Sunflower	*Helianthus annus*
Sweet Cicely	*Myrrhis odorata*
Sweet-flag	*Acorus calamus*
Tansy	*Tanacetum vulgare*
Tarragon (French)	*Artemisia dracunculus*
Thistle, Milk	*Silybum marianum*
Thyme	*Thymus vulgaris*
Thyme, Golden	*Thymus vulgaris v. aureus*
Thyme, Lemon	*Thymus x citriodorus*
Tormentil	*Potentilla erecta*
Valerian, Common	*Valeriana officinalis*
Verbena	*Verbena officinalis*
Verbena, Lemon	*Aloysia triphylla*
Vervain	*Verbena officinalis*
Vetch, Tuberous	*Lathyrus linifolius* C
Violet, Sweet	*Viola odorata*
Viper's-bugloss	*Echium vulgare*
Water-lily, White	*Nymphea alba*
Weld	*Reseda luteola*
Willows	*Salix*
Wintergreen, False	*Gaultheria procumbens*
Witch Hazel	*Hamamelis molis*
Witch Hazel, Virginian	*Hamamelis virginiana*
Woad	*satis tinctoria*
Wood Avens	*Geum urbanum*
Woodruff	*Galium odoratum*
Wormwood	*Artemisia absinthium*
Wormwood, Roman	*Artemisia ponticum*
Woundwort, Marsh	*Stachys palustris*
Yarrow	*Achillea millefolium*
Yew	*Taxus baccata*

A Garden of Herbs

Glossary

Abortifacient	A substance which causes abortion
Alimentary canal	Digestive tract from mouth to anus
Alkaloids	Bitter, often based on plant compounds that contain nitrogen *eg* caffeine. Some are toxic and addictive
Allergic reactions	Sensitive reactions in some people to different stimuli causing asthma, skin reactions etc.
Analgesic	Pain reducing substance
Anti-coagulant	Prevents blood clotting
Anti-inflammatory	Reduces inflammation
Anti-oxidants	Compounds which scavenge free radicals
Antispasmodic	Relieves muscle spasm
Aphrodisiac	Promotes sexual excitement
Astringent	Tightens mucus membranes and skin, reducing secretions and bleeding
Atropine	A toxic alkaloid obtained from *Atropa belladonna* deadly nightshade and other members of the Solanaceae family
Ayurveda	Traditional Indian medicine
Azulenes	Volatile oils present in some plants
Bitter	Stimulates secretions of saliva and digestive juices, increasing appetite
Carminative	Relieves flatulence and indigestion
Carotenes	Reddish-yellow pigments, can be converted to vitamin A by animal tissue
Coumarins	Antibacterial, anticoagulant, with a smell of new-mown hay, noticed in cut grasses
Decoction	Water-based preparation of bark, roots, berries or seeds simmered in boiling water
Demulcent	Smooth and soothing when applied to sore or inflamed or painful surface
Detoxification	The process of removing toxins from the body

Diuretic	Stimulates urine volume and flow
Dropsy	An old-fashioned term for heart failure by accumulation of fluid in body tissue
Emetic	Causes vomiting
Emollient	Softens and smoothes the skin
Essential oils	Volatile plant oils – often scented of the plant, obtained by distillation
Flavonoids	A group of chemicals found in some plants in very high concentration, thought to be important dietary anti-oxidants
Gastro-intestinal tract	Alimentary system
Glycosyides	Compounds with one or more sugar groups attached
HIV	Human Immune Deficiency
Hyoscyamine	A toxic alkaloid
Hypertension	High blood pressure
Hypoglycaemia	Abnormally low blood glucose levels
Immunology	The study of how the body responds to foreign matter that may cause damage or infection
Immune stimulant	Stimulates the body's immune defences to fight infection
Immuno-suppressant	Suppresses the body's defences to fight infection
Infusion	Water-based preparation in which flowers, leaves or stems are brewed like tea
Latex	Milky juice or sap produced by stems or other organs when cut
Leukaemia	Tumor of the white blood cells
Lymphoma	Tumor of the lymph glands
Mucilage	Bland, slimy, and soothing substance, present in some plants. Some give help to inflamed surfaces
Opium	A dried exudate from opium poppy
Phototoxic	Reactions activated by sunshine
Steroids	Active chemicals with powerful hormonal action
Tincture	A solution extracted from plants with alcohol or water-alcohol solution
Tisane	A drink made by adding boiling water to plant material, often leaves
Volatile oils	Aromatic oils, may be antiseptic, irritant or fungicidal
Vulnerary	A substance used to treat or heals wounds

A Garden of Herbs

Bibliography

1. Apicius (1958) *The Roman Cookery Book* tr. B.& E Rosenbaum, Harrap & Co, London
2. Bannerman, J. (1986) *The Beatons: A medical kindred in the classical Gaelic tradition* John Donald, Edinburgh
3. Barnes, J. Anderson, L.A. & Phillipson. J.D. (2002) *Herbal Medicines – A Guide for Health-care Professionals* (Second edition) The Pharmaceutical Press, London
4. Beaton (1563) *Regimen Sanitatus* Ms English translation Gillies, H.C. (1911) Ref Gaelic Medicine, Glasgow Libraries
5. Beith, M. (1995) *Healing threads* Polygon, Edinburgh
6. Boney, A. D. (1988) *The Lost Gardens of Glasgow University* Christopher Helm Ltd, Kent
7. Bown, D. (1995) *Encyclopedia of Herbs and their Uses* Royal Horticultural Society Dorling Kindersley, London
8. Boxer, A. & Black, P. (1980) *The Herb Book* Octopus Books Ltd. London
9. Bremness, L. (2000) *Fragrance for mind, body & spirit* Herbs Vol. 25 No. 3 The Herb Society, Oxon.
10. Burton, R. (1994) *Proteins, Ancient Greeks and T'ang Poetry* Polygon, Edinburgh
11. Cameron, J. (1883) *The Gaelic names of plants* William Blackwood & Sons, Edinburgh
12. Chevallier, A (1996) *The Encyclopaedia of Medicinal Plants* Dorling Kindersley, London
13. Darwin, T. (1996) *The Scots herbal: The plant lore of Scotland* Mercat Press, Edinburgh
14. Dickson, C. & Dickson, J.H. (2001) *Plants and People in Ancient Scotland* Tempus Publishing Ltd, Gloucestershire
15. Dickson, J.H. & Gauld, W. W. (1987) *Mark Jameson's Physic Plants, A Sixteenth Century Garden for Gynaocology in Glasgow?* Scottish Medical Journal, Vol. 32
16. Edmonstone, T. (1841) *On the dyes of the Shetland Isles* Transactions of the Botanical Society, Edinburgh
17. Fairweather, B. (undated *c.*1984). *Highland plant lore* Glencoe and North Lorne Folk Museum, Glencoe
18. Genders, R. (1977) *Scented Flora of the World* Robert Hale Ltd, London

19. Genders, R. (1971) *The Scented Wild Flowers of Britain* Collins, London

20. Gerard, J. (1597) *The Herball or Generall Historie of Plantes*

21. Geyer-Kordesch, J. & Macdonald, F. (1999) *History of the Royal College of Physicians and Surgeons of Glasgow, 1599-1858* The Hambledon Press, London

22. Giacosa, I. (1992) *A Taste of Ancient Rome* University of Chicago Press, Chicago & London

23. Grant, I. F. (1961) *Highland Folk Ways* Routledge & Keagan Paul, London

24. Grieve, M. (ed . Leyel, C.F.) (1992) *A Modern Herbal* Tiger Books International, London

25. Grierson, S. (1986) *The colour cauldron* Published privately, Mill Books, Tibbermore, Perth

26. Grigson, G. (1958) *The Englishman's Flora* Paladin, St Albans, Herts.

27. Harper, J.(undated) *How to Choose a Herbal Medicine for you* In association with Solgar Vitamins, www.Solgar.com.uk

28.. Henderson, D. M. & Dickson, J. H. (1994) *A naturalist in the Highlands* (James Robertson, his life and travels in Scotland) Scottish Academic Press

29. Harvey, J. (1981) *Medieval Gardens* Batsford, London

30. Henslow, G. (1905) *The Uses of British plants* Lovell, Reeve & Co, London

31. Johnson, C. P. & Sowerby, J. E. (1862) *The useful plants of Great Britain* Robert Hardwicke, London

32. Kenicer, G. *Flora Celtica* Exhibition produced for the Royal Botanic Gardens, Edinburgh

33. Lawson, P. (1852) *Vegetable products of Scotland* Private Press

34. Lewis, W. H. & Elvin-Lewis, M.P. F. (1977) *Medical Botany – Plants affecting Man's Health* John Wiley & Sons, London

35. Lightfoot, J. (1777) *Flora Scotica* White, London

36. MacIntyre, A. (1997) *The Apothecary's Garden* Judy Piatkus Ltd, London

37. MacIntyre, D. (1999) *The role of Scottish native plants in natural dyeing and textiles* MSc thesis University of Edinburgh, Institute of Ecology and Resource Management

38. Macpherson, P. (1982) *The Doctrine of Signatures* Glasgow Naturalist, Vol. 20 part 3

39. Mabey, R. (1996) *Flora Britannica* Sinclair-Stevenson, London

40. Mahon, L. (undated) (In association with Bioforce Research) *Herbs for Healthy Living*

41. Manniche, L. (1993) *An Ancient Egyptian Herbal* British Museum Press, London

42. Martin, M. (1994) *A description of the Western Isles of Scotland circa 1695* (Reprinted edition by Macleod, D.J.) Birlinn, Edinburgh

43. Mills, S. & Bone, K. (2000) *Principles and Practice of Phytotherapy* Churchill Livingstone, London

44. Newall, C. Anderson, L. & Philipson, (1996) *Herbal Medicines – A Guide for Health-care Professionals* The Pharmacutical Press, London

45. Nicolson, A. (1958) *The McBeths – Hereditary Physicians of the Highlands* Transactions of the Gaelic Society ofGlasgow Vol. 5

46. Pennant, T. (1959) *A Tour in Scotland, 1779* (facsimile of 3rd edition) Melvin Press, Perth

47. Ross, A. (1974) *Scottish Home Industries* (1895) Molendinar, Glasgow

48. School of Scottish Studies, University of Edinburgh, Oral history, various sources

49. Schetky, E.McD. (1982) *The Ageless Art of Dyeing* Plants & Gardens Vol. 20, No. 3 Brooklyn Botanic Garden, Brooklyn NY

50. Shaw, M. F. (1955) *Folksongs and folklore of South Uist* Routledge, Kegan & Paul, London

51. Sowerby, J. E. & Johnson, C.P. (1863) *British Wild Flowers* John Van Voorst, London

52. Stace, C. (1997) *New Flora of the British Isles* (2nd edit.) Cambridge University Press, Cambridge

53. Stockwell, C. (1989) *Nature's Pharmacy* Arrow Books, London, Published in Association with the Royal Botanic Gardens, Kew

54. Stuart, M. ed. (1987) *The Encyclopaedia of Herbs and Herbalism* MacDonald & Co. Ltd, London

55. Sumner, J. (2000) *The Natural History of Medicinal Plants* Timber Press Inc, Portland, Oregon

56. Thompson, F. (1969) *Harris tweed – The Story of a Hebridean Industry* David & Charles, London

57. Vickery, C. R. (1995) *A dictionary of plant lore* Oxford University Press, Oxford

58. Wickham-Jones, C. R. (1990) *Rhum: Mesolithic and later sites at Kinloch* Society of Antiquaries of Scotland Monograph series: 7

59. www.rbge.org.uk *The Scots Herbal: Uses of Native Scottish Plants*

Index

A Garden of Herbs